Copyright 1988   ISO-GALAGO.

Prepared for publication by
ISO PUBLICATIONS
137 Westminster Bridge Road,
London SE1 7HR.
Tel. 01-261-9588/9179.

Published jointly with GALAGO Publishing Ltd
of 42 Palace Grove, Bromley, Kent BR1 3HB.
Tel. 01-290-0245.

ISBN 0 946784 95 7

The Jeep
Its Development & Procurement
under the Quartermaster Corps, 1940-1943

by Herbert R. Rifkind

ISO-GALAGO

**THE JEEP—ITS DEVELOPMENT AND PROCUREMENT
UNDER THE QUARTERMASTER CORPS, 1940-1942**

by

Herbert R. Rifkind

Historical Section
General Service Branch
General Adminstrative Services
Office of the Quartermaster General

Washington, DC

1943

Filmset in Optima by
AMR Typesetting, Smallfield, Surrey.

ISO Publications, London, England

1988

Contents

List of Illustrations

Introduction

For a vehicle as small and new to the military scene as the Army's now well-known "jeep,"[1] this "truck, ¼-ton, 4x4," as it is officially designated, has been the cause of considerable controversy during its short career. The history of its development and procurement under the auspices of the Quartermaster Corps from 1940 to 1942 has been almost as violent as its subsequent acrobatics in the role of a command-reconnaissance car and light weapons carrier on the field of battle.

While the jeep was probably the most spectacular accomplishment of the QMC and one of the outstanding successes of any of the supply services of the Army in the present war, its conception and birth were not achieved without travail. In the beginning, this took the form of a dispute between the using arms, as represented by the Infantry, Field Artillery, and Cavalry, and the Quartermaster Corps, the supply service charged with the development and procurement of the jeep as well as all other general purpose vehicles. Most of the contention took place over the always important matter of having to reconcile the vehicular military characteristics as conceived by the using arms, with the specifications, the writing of which was the responsibility of the QMC. The weight of the proposed vehicle, for instance, was a principal point of conflict. The using arms were determined that their original concept of a light car to replace the motorcycle with sidecar and capable of being handled by a three-man crew, should be adhered to as closely as possible, while the QMC Motor Transport Division, from its long experience in automotive matters, realised that no four-wheeled vehicle could possibly be built to the original 1200 pound weight limit set by the using arms and still perform as desired or take the punishment it was bound to receive in carrying out its cross-country missions.

When the testing period for the jeep was over, and it was seen that it was a lusty youngster, another argument ensued, this time over the question of who originated and developed it and to whom the credit should go. Army protagonists claimed that the Army was primarily responsible for the jeep's development, a claim that was disputed by the American Bantam Car Company, which built the first successful models and regarded the jeep as its "baby". Later, when the Willys-Overland model of the jeep was chosen for standardisation and mass production, that company embarked on an advertising campaign in which it intimated that Willys' engineers were the real creators of the jeep. Whereupon the Willys concern was pounced upon by that watchdog of the advertising pages, the Federal Trade Commission, which issued a complaint against it for fraudulent advertising. The brief holding that American Bantam in collaboration with certain Army officers, and not Willys, had originated the jeep. Even today, the question of who developed the jeep is a matter that is still being debated.

The ever-mounting estimates of requirements that would be needed for a vehicle such as the jeep in the event of war—a probability that was looming larger and larger in 1940 and 1941—forecast for it a rapid growth and robust future. With the jeep's place in the Army's sun thus seemingly assured, a scramble for jeep contracts took place between American Bantam, Willys, and Ford. To these three automobile manufacturers not only were the immediate contracts important, but the post-war commercial potentialities of this little vehicle, which had so captivated public fancy, also bulked largely in their minds.

The competition for the early jeep contracts soon involved the whole War Department from the Offices of the Secretary and Under Secretary of War down through the infantry, Field Artillery, Cavalry, and the Quartermaster Corps. The Office of Production Management also had a hand in this procurement controversy. It seemed as if everyone took sides—the using arms at first backing American Bantam, while the Quartermaster Corps wished to bring Ford and Willys into the picture as well. The QMC especially looked with favour upon Ford whom it naturally regarded as the "largest and most dependable" producer, thus bringing down upon itself denunciations from the pro-labour press for its attitude. The battle for contracts see-sawed through the fall of 1940 and into the summer of 1941. When the smoke finally lifted, and it was seen that the American Bantam, the alleged "small-business" underdog in this competition, had been eliminated from the production program of the jeep—Willys and Ford later splitting the jeep contracts on a fifty-fifty basis—another uproar arose that carried to the portals of Congress. In August 1941, the Truman Committee subjected the entire jeep affair to an investigation, at which War Department and Quartermaster motor procurement policies and methods were gone into at length.

During all this furore, research had been going ahead on an amphibious counterpart of the jeep. Although this amphibian jeep was still not in production at the time of the transfer of all motor transport activities from the Quartermaster Corps to the Ordnance Department in the summer of 1942, much progress had been made in its development and later in the year these motor boat hulls built around the jeep chassis began to roll off the Ford assembly line. When the final reports were in from Sicily, Italy and other war theatres where the amphibian jeep participated in invasion and landing operations in 1943, this aquatic version of the jeep was found as sterling a performer on sea as its dynamic older brother had proven to be on land.

The whole story of the jeep, aside from being an interesting and colourful narrative in itself, is important historically. Among the many individual contributions of the Quartermaster Corps to the present war effort, the jeep, perhaps, has been the most significant. Furthermore, it is believed that this monograph on the jeep, though incomplete in many respects, has a definite value in that it illustrates the more essential procedures and operations by which motor vehicles were developed and procured by the Quartermaster Corps during the time such functions were under its jurisdiction.

In addition to the operational side of the story, an attempt has been made, mainly through the use of footnotes, to outline the chief policy developments behind the operations so as to provide as much background and orientation as possible without unduly disrupting the continuity of the narrative. The account presented in the following pages was prepared almost entirely from official records and other documents in the Office of the Quartermaster General, copies of which are on file in the Historical Section of the General Administrative Services Division.

NOTES to INTRODUCTION

1   The origin and meaning of the word "jeep" are not too certain. Writing in reply to a query on this subject from the Editor of the Winston Dictionaries, Philadelphia, Pa, the QMC Motor Transport Division on 30 October 1941 stated: "The word 'jeep' has no official military status, but over a long period of years has come to mean to Army men a new type of military motor vehicle." The Editor was informed that until the advent of the $\frac{1}{4}$-ton truck the word had been generally applied to the $\frac{1}{2}$-ton, 4x4, used for command reconnaissance and general cargo purposes. When the $\frac{1}{4}$-ton made its debut, it was variously dubbed "jeep" "baby jeep," and "peep". During the 1941 manoeuvres, it was said that Army mechanics and others generally came to refer to it as the "peep," to distinguish it from the $\frac{1}{2}$-ton "jeep". *QM 095 M-A (Winston, John C, Co) Major G.H. Vogel to Thomas K. Brown, Jr, Editor, The Winston Dictionaries, 30 October 1941.*

Other names attached to the $\frac{1}{4}$-ton about this time were "jeepie", "son-of-a-jeep", "blitz-buggy", "bantam", "puddle jumper", etc.

Another explanation of the word "jeep" is that it originated from the slurring of the initial letters of the War Department's vehicle classification "general purpose" (G.P.), under which the $\frac{1}{4}$-ton was listed, into a single monosyllable. Credence is lent this theory by the fact that an early spelling variation of the word was "geep". Regardless of how the name originated, after a $\frac{3}{4}$-ton model was developed late in 1941 to replace the $\frac{1}{2}$-ton truck, the title of "jeep" was settled permanently on the $\frac{1}{4}$-ton, apparently by common consent. On 19 February 1942, Lt. Col. Edwin S. Van Deusen, MT Chief of Procurement and Engineering, speaking before the Metropolitan Chapter, Society of Automotive Engineers, New York City, said that the $\frac{1}{4}$-ton was "affectionately known to millions now as the 'jeep'."

CHAPTER I

Origin and Development of the Jeep

Early Predecessors:

The Austin
Despite the lack of funds for research and development which severely handicapped the Army in the depression decade before the present-day jeep came into being, both the Quartermaster Corps and other service branches—notably the Infantry—were alive to the need for a light weight vehicle to replace the motorcycle, particularly for cross country use. The motorcycle, even when equipped with a sidecar, was recognised as a notoriously poor performer in this regard and dangerous to operate off the road except in the hands of a most expert rider. It was strongly felt that a machine was needed for reconnaissance and motor messenger service which could be operated effectively under all conditions.

Accordingly, in November 1932, the Infantry Board, that service's own branch for developing and testing infantry equipment, recommended to the Chief of Infantry that an Austin[1] roadster with oversized tyres be procured and sent to the Board at Fort Benning, Georgia, for test. In its memorandum the Board pointed out the deficiencies of the motorcycle and called attention to "extensive and highly satisfactory use of Austin cars in the British Army for reconnaissance and messenger service." The Quartermaster General's Office, to which the request for the purchase of the Austin had been forwarded, while appreciating the desirability of testing this vehicle, was forced to reply that no funds were available to purchase it since "the Army Appropriation Act did not authorize the purchase of any automobiles for the Regular Army during the present fiscal year." In the following month, however, the War Department authorized the purchase, from funds specially allotted to The Quartermaster General, of one or two Austins of the reconnaissance truck type, carrying two passengers and having a pick-up body. The one Austin that was eventually purchased, at a cost of $286.75[2], while a far cry from the ultimate jeep, served the useful purpose of indicating to the Army what it might expect in the way of performance from a small car.[3]

The Howie Machine-gun Carrier

In addition to the need for an effective substitute for the motorcycle for cross country reconnaissance and messenger purposes, the Army for a long time had been faced with another problem that was somewhat similar—that of providing a light weapons carrier to give quick and close support to attacking infantry. Writing of this problem in the *Infantry Journal,* November-December 1937, Captain Wendell G. Johnson pointed out that none of the orthodox methods in use up to that time had proved satisfactory. The trucks of the day, because of their size, were too vulnerable to enemy fire, while the time-honoured alternate method of hand-hauling by sweating, cussing privates crawling along the ground from one firing position to another was too slow. Moreover, the task of lugging the Army's heavy .50-calibre machine gun, the largest calibre employed by any military service in the world, was simply beyond the muscle power of even the huskiest soldier.

Officers concerned with this problem knew that something else would have to be devised to fit in with the growing concept of modern, high-speed, mechanized warfare. From these critics of the immobility of supporting weapons, said Johnson, there arose a demand for a motorized carrier, a vehicle that would be extremely low in silhouette, that would carry a one or two-man crew, with a gun and plenty of ammunition, and which would be able to "scoot from one firing position to another at five to ten miles an hour." In 1936, Brigadier General Walter C. Short, Assistant Commandant of the Infantry School at Fort Benning, Georgia, ordered the construction of a vehicle with the above characteristics. Additional requirements specified by General Short were that the .30-calibre machine gun to be carried was not to be mounted for firing from the carrier; the vehicle was to be light enough for four men to manhandle over small obstacles and lift into the 1½-ton truck issued to machine-gun companies; and the units used were to be commercially available as far as possible. Designed and built by Captain Robert G. Howie, with Master Sergeant M.C. Wiley as his partner in production, the job was finished in April 1937, Sergeant G.L. Rush assisting in the final assembly. All of these men were from the Infantry School's Tank Section where Captain Howie was then serving as an instructor. The completed vehicle, naturally enough, became known as the Howie Machine-Gun Carrier.[4]

The only vehicle of its kind ever designed and built by the Army, the Howie Machine-Gun Carrier, like the earlier Austin, differed materially from the jeep of 1940-1941 both in appearance and construction, judging from a comparison of Captain Johnson's description of the carrier with 1941 specifications of the jeep. One of the singular differences in appearance was due to the prone position assumed on the Howie machine by its two-man crew, in contrast to the upright seated position normally taken by the occupants of the later jeep. The Howie Carrier had no body with bucket or cross seats as did the jeep. Lying flat on their stomachs on a sort of bed over the chassis of the Howie machine, or turned partially sideways, the two crew members operated and steered the vehicle from this position.

Captain Howie's report on his carrier, as quoted in Johnson's article, stated it had been decided "that in order to provide a low silhouette, the crew should be placed in the prone position." This, it was thought "should assist in determining the feasibility of this feature for future designs." The whole ensemble thus presented a very low silhouette, considerably lower in fact than the later ¼-ton models. According to Captain Johnson, this feature made the Howie Machine-Gun Carrier practically invisible in the tests "even on flat terrain with little vegetation to provide cover." A machine gunner, upon seeing the carrier perform, was reported to have said: "Jees, she's lower'n the grass. You can't hardly see her even when she's going."

The over-all height of the Howie Carrier was 33¼ inches as compared with the 40-inch silhouette height (body proper, cowl and hood) specified for the jeep in 1941. Comparison of other dimensions reveal that in general Captain Howie's vehicle was smaller than the jeep, weighed far less, and scarcely matched the jeep's performance ability. The wheelbase of the Howie Carrier was 75 inches, five less than the jeep's 80; its weight, less machine gun and equipment was 1,015 pounds compared to the final weight of the standardised jeep of well over a ton; and its maximum speed was 28 miles per hour, whereas the jeep had no difficulty in hitting a mile-a-minute pace.[5]

Construction features of the Howie Machine-Gun Carrier were also quite different from those of its ¼-ton successor. Some salvaged Austin parts from the Fort Benning salvage pile—perhaps the very ones that composed the Austin purchased in 1932—were used in the building of the machine. These included the radiator, steering gear and probably the propeller shaft, universal joints, and rear axle assembly. A new Austin engine, weighing 155 pounds with clutch and transmission, was used for the job and placed in the rear of the vehicle, because of the nature of the drive Howie planned to employ. This engine position, of course, was the opposite of the conventional front mounting of the jeep's engine. The propeller shaft was modified by shortening and the rear axle assembly was reversed in order to provide for the unusual reversal-in-drive system that was used. The rear axle formed a jackshaft mounted amidships and an 11-tooth sprocket fitted to the ends of the shaft operated a standard motorcycle chain to a 21-tooth motorcycle sprocket on the rear wheels, thus giving an additional and necessary gear reduction of 2 to 1. No four-wheel drive, as in the jeep, was employed. Instead of the usual steering wheel, the Howie machine was steered by a tiller arrangement. It also had no springs.[6]

When tested in the field, Captain Johnson reported that the Howie Carrier performed exceptionally well for an experimental model. It was able to carry with ease the 81 mm mortar, the .50-calibre machine gun, and the 37 mm anti-tank and anti-aircraft gun; the latter weapon also was towed without difficulty. In the hands of Lieutenant Charles R. Kutz and personnel of Company D, 29th Infantry, it ran through puddles without baulking or stalling and "charged through light underbrush in a fashion that made even designer Howie's eyes pop." Its 6.00 x 9 tractor tyres, broad in relation to the vehicle's low weight, gave it excellent flotation on sand in which other vehicles sank or wallowed.[7] A few years later, the Libyan campaigns of North Africa were to demonstrate that proper flotation for desert operations could be better obtained from huge, oversized, single tyres rather than from the ordinary dual tyre equipment with which American commercial vehicles were equipped. Later desert tests conducted by the QMC Motor Transport Division in Southern California were to confirm this.

While both the Austin and Howie Carrier thus may be regarded as predecessors of the jeep, it appears doubtful whether either can be considered its prototype. The first was experimented with as a reconnaissance car substituting for the motorcycle, while the Howie machine was designed strictly as a light, low-silhouette weapons carrier. The problem now was to combine these two functions into a single vehicle. The first steps in this direction were to be taken by the Chiefs of Infantry and Cavalry, and the basis of the development was to be the commercial Bantam car manufactured by the American Bantam Car Company of Butler, Pennsylvania, successors to the former American Austin Company at the same location. Captain Howie, among others, was to be a consultant in the initial stages of this project.

Development of the Jeep, 1940

General Development Procedure
Before undertaking to trace the development of the present day jeep, it is desirable for purposes of orientation that a general understanding be had of the process by which motor vehicles were developed for the Army around this time particularly in regard to the development functions of the Quartermaster Corps. Ideas for new developments could originate in many sources: from the using arms and services in the field, each of which maintained its own test board (such as the Infantry Board) for the purpose of originating designs and equipment peculiar to its own requirements; in the engineering branch of the Quartermaster Corps' own Motor Transport Division[8]; by civilian inventors, whose ideas were channelled through the National Inventors' Council; or by manufacturers submitting their proposals directly.

The first step in any new motor vehicle development was the preparation of a general statement of desirable military characteristics; this was the responsibility of the using arm. After approval of the project by the General Staff, representing the Secretary of War[9], the Office of The Quartermaster General was directed to proceed with the development.

Under Army regulations, the responsibility of the Quartermaster Corps in regard to the development and procurement of motor vehicles was limited to the general purpose type—motor vehicles used for the general hauling of cargo, ammunition, personnel, or equipment. Combat or fighting vehicles such as tanks or armoured cars, on the other hand, came under the jurisdiction of the Ordnance Department[10]. Quartermaster vehicles were further divided into two general classes: administrative and tactical. Administrative vehicles, which closely paralleled the normal commercial product, were used for housekeeping purposes in the zone of the interior. Tactical vehicles, distinguished from the administrative type by always having the all-wheel drive[11]—the oustanding difference between the military and commercial truck—filled the requirements of the field forces for the transporting of supplies, personnel, and equipment under combat or manoeuvre conditions. It was primarily as a tactical vehicle that the jeep was developed, although its remarkable versatility has caused it to be used for a host of administrative purposes as well.

After receipt of the directive from the General Staff approving the development of a new general purpose vehicle, the project had to be reviewed and approved by the QMC Technical Committee, which included in its membership representatives from all of the arms and services. In the case of motor items, the development was first considered by a Motor Transport subcommittee which reported to the Technical Committee as a whole. It was the function of the Technical Committee to co-ordinate, and, if necessary, revise the military characteristics when a vehicle was to be used by several of the arms and services. In many instances differences of opinion arose between the different using arms or between the using arms and the Quartermaster representative. Frequently, difficult compromises had to be made in instances where certain features of a vehicle were advantageous to one service branch and disadvantageous to another. In the case of the jeep, as has already been noted, the disagreement was between the using arms and the Quartermaster Corps, principally over the characteristic of weight, but also over other issues revolving about War Department and Quartermaster policies, which will be discussed later.

FLOW CHART

War Departmental Functional Relationships in development of a motor vehicle

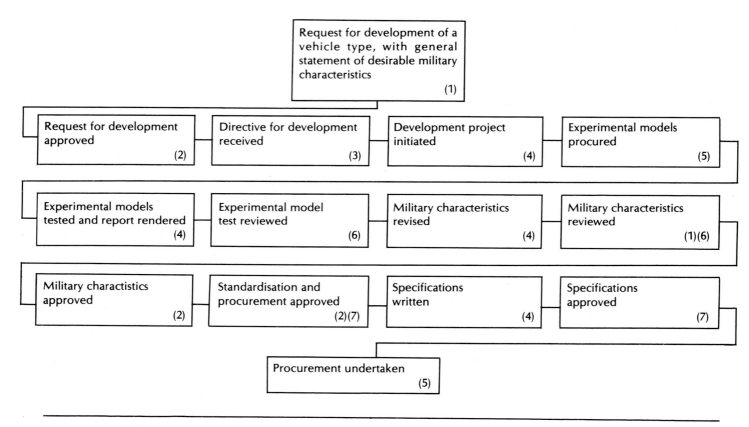

Request for development of a vehicle type, with general statement of desirable military characteristics (1)

Request for development approved (2)	Directive for development received (3)	Development project initiated (4)	Experimental models procured (5)
Experimental models tested and report rendered (4)	Experimental model test reviewed (6)	Military characteristics revised (4)	Military characteristics reviewed (1)(6)
Military charactistics approved (2)	Standardisation and procurement approved (2)(7)	Specifications written (4)	Specifications approved (7)

Procurement undertaken (5)

Legend

(1)   Using Arms and Services
(2)   General Staff (later, by SOS)
(3)   Office of the Quartermaster General
(4)   OQMG Motor Transport Division (Engineering)

(5)   OQMG Motor Transport Division (Procurement)
(6)   QMC Technical Committee
        (through Motor Subcommittee)
(7)   Assistant Secretary of War (later, the ......

When the military characteristics were finally approved by majority vote of the QMC Technical Committee, they were again sent to the General Staff for the Secretary of War's approval. With the receipt of the Secretary's confirming endorsement, the QMC directed its Motor Transport Division to write specifications that would include in every detail the military characteristics of the proposed vehicle.[11] This was accomplished by the Motor Transport Engineering Branch located at the Holabird Quartermaster Depot, Baltimore, Maryland, where the motor development and procurement activities were concentrated at the time. The prepared specifications were then reviewed and approved by the Assistant Secretary of War (later the Under Secretary of War) who, ever since the passage of the National Defence Act in 1920, had been charged with the responsibility for all War Department procurements. After receipt of the Assistant Secretary of War's approval of the specifications, the Office of The Quartermaster General directed the Motor Transport Procurement Branch, also located at Holabird, to initiate the purchase of the vehicle. Before a manufacturer was permitted to go into production, however, a pilot model had to be made up and submitted to Holabird for an acceptance test.[12]

The Original Bantam Development

In the period between the Howie Machine-Gun Carrier and the new conception of the jeep, the Army had been experimenting, somewhat unsatisfactorily, with extra light models of the regular 1½-ton, 4x4, cargo trucks. Thirty-nine of these vehicles were tested by the Infantry around 1938 for suitability as weapons carriers over cross-country terrain under adverse weather conditions, and for manhandling properties. These proving unsatisfactory, a still lighter ½-ton, 4x4, pickup was purchased, and this vehicle, while its cost was approximately the same as the 1½-ton, 4x4, was found to be a vast improvement. The Motor Transport subcommittee discovered in the ½-ton, distinct advantages of lighter weight, better flotation, and greater cross-country ability. The Quartermaster Technical Committee, therefore, recommended that experimentation with the stripped version of the 1½-ton truck cease and that its military characteristics be cancelled; at the same time it voted that the ½-ton be adopted as a standard model. Both of these recommendations were approved by the Secretary of War.[13]

But the ½-ton truck, while a useful vehicle for many purposes, was still virtually an outright commercial model, unsuitable to the command and reconnaissance light-car idea the Infantry and Cavalry had in mind.[14] By 1940 the Chief of Infantry again emphasised to the War Department: "Facilities available to organizations for increased speed in tactical employment of infantry units, including development of more rapid means of communication within the infantry battalion, demand greater mobility for platoon leaders of the Heavy Weapons Company and cross-country ability for motorcycle messengers." The ½-ton used by company commanders and platoon leaders was held to be a much larger vehicle than required. Moreover, its weight and relatively high silhouette made it unsuitable for company and platoon commanders, whose duties in combat, involving movement in close proximity to opposing forces, required a vehicle capable of being manhandled by two men if necessary, and having a minimum silhouette.

Once more pointing out that the motorcycle was not efficient for this purpose, the Chief of Infantry set up a requirement for a vehicle that was to have a maximum height and weight of 36 inches and 750-1000lbs; cross-country and grade ability equal to that of standard cargo vehicles; either an integral or detachable .30 calibre machine gun mount; capacity for at least two men, one machine gun including accessories, and 3,000 rounds of ammunition; low silhouette; and four-wheel drive. If feasible, and if the production of test vehicles would not be unduly delayed, the frame and body were to be designed so as to provide amphibious characteristics; if prevailing conditions made it impossible to incorporate this feature at the time it was desired that experimentation and development along that line be continued until brought to a successful conclusion.[15] Thus it can be seen that the concept of an amphibious complement to the light reconnaissance car was born simultaneously with the land model idea.

When the proposed development was forwarded to the Quartermaster General by the AGO, for comment and recommendation,[17] the Quartermaster General viewed the chassis development, since the requirement was for command-reconnaissance purposes (hence "general purpose" as well as "combat"), as one that should be the responsibility of his office (rather than Ordnance) and suggested that Holabird investigate the light passenger car of the American Bantam Company as a possible solution of the problem.[18] At the same time, the Ordnance Department, through its own Technical Committee, entered the proceedings because of its connection with the Howie Machine-Gun Carrier developed by the Tank Section personnel at the Infantry School at Ft. Benning, Georgia.

Athough the Howie Carrier, since its construction in 1937, had been variously tested and demonstrated, no concrete plans for its production had ever been made by the War Department or anyone else.[19] Now, however, the Chief of Ordnance was being directed by the General Staff to give further consideration to the Howie vehicle. The command-reconnaissance proposal of the Infantry and Cavalry, therefore, was forwarded to the Ordnance Department for appropriate action and recommendation through its Technical Committee, the idea being to investigate thoroughly both possibilities at the same time. In this connection, the Chief of Ordnance was asked by the Adjutant General to consider the Bantam car manufactured by the American Bantam Car Company. A subcommittee was to be appointed by the Chief of Ordnance to look into the matter; in addition to whatever Ordnance personnel he wished to designate; it was to include representatives from the Infantry, Cavalry and Office of the Quartermaster General.[20]

On 19 June 1940, a special subcommittee and Major Howie, whose presence had been requested by the subcommittee so that he could give full information on his carrier, met with officials and engineers of the Bantam Company at their Butler, Pennsylvania plant for discussion of the possibilities and limitations of the Bantam chassis as a basis for both the proposed command-reconnaissance car and the Howie Weapons Carrier. Several of the regular Bantam 2-wheel drive cars were put through a brief test, including runs over hilly country with grades estimated at ten per cent. Carrying one or two men, and with a gross load of approximately 1,500 pounds, they performed well. To test the car's structural strength, a stripped, dry chassis weighing 680 pounds, was statically loaded with 4,500 pounds of sand without damage to the chassis.[21]

A discussion of engineering details followed resulting in a tentative decision to require, among other things, a driving front axle with a 2-speed transfer case including provision for disengaging the front axle drive; a body of rectangular design with folding windshield and three bucket seats; increased engine power; means for towing; a .30-calibre machine gun mount on a telescoping pedestal; blackout lighting and oil-bath air cleaner; and such regularly accepted components in the automobile industry as hydraulic brakes and full floating axles. Based on the recommendations of the using arms, a modified set of military characteristics was drawn up that limited the weight to a maximum of 1,200 pounds; the wheel base to approximately 75 inches and the maximum height to 36 inches. Angles of approach and departure were set at 45° and 40° respectively, and a speed range on level, hard surface of three to not less than 50 miles per hour was required.[22]

The Chief of Infantry, in his recommendation to the General Staff, stated that enough vehicles generally conforming to the above characteristics should be procured as would enable the equipment of one infantry rifle regiment with such units for extended service test, and six additional for the Infantry Board—40 vehicles in all. Recognising that the desired type was impracticable of development from the current commercial trucks of the day, he further urged that the competitive bidding regulations then in force for the procurement of Army trucks be waived to the extent necessary for the development of the possible design. The Chief of Cavalry concurred in all of these recommendations, requesting that he be kept informed of the development, and that 20 of the manufactured vehicles be assigned to him for test.[16]

The subcommittee viewed the development of the proposed reconnaissance car and the Howie Weapons Carrier as being essentially the same. Apart from the prone position of the operator, if the Howie Carrier was to operate in convoy with other vehicles it would have to be equipped with conventional steering and brake and clutch controls; otherwise it would have to be transported in trucks. In future tests of the proposed Bantam development, which it was thought should be limited solely to the light reconnaissance and command car type, the subcommittee foresaw the answer to whether any further experimentation of the light reconnaissance car or the Howie Weapons Carrier should be undertaken. Accordingly, it recommended the adoption of the military characteristics it had drawn up and the procurement of 70 of these cars for service testing by the using arms—40 for the Infantry, 20 for the Cavalry and 10 for the Field Artillery. Because this vehicle was to be of the commercial wheeled type without armour, thus falling within the "general purpose" classification, the subcommittee recommended that the Quartermaster Corps be charged with its development and procurement, and that if the truck proved satisfactory, consideration should be given to its use as a substitute for the motorcycle with sidecar.[23]

Approval of the Ordnance subcommittee's report and recommendations was quickly forthcoming from the Secretary of War and the expenditure of not more than $175,000 of Quartermaster funds was authorised for the project, with the vehicles to be ready in time for the late-summer manoeuvres of 1940, if possible. Following testing under the supervision of the using arm's test boards, their findings were to be co-ordinated by the Quartermaster Technical Committee after which final recommendations were to be submitted by the Quartermaster General to the Secretary of War[24]. The tentative specifications, dated 2 July, set forth in detail the service requirements of the vehicle and contained some specification changes agreed to by the representatives of the Infantry and Cavalry at a Holabird conference on 1 July. The weight was raised seventy-five pounds to 1,275, the maximum wheelbase was increased to 80 inches, and the overall height of the truck was raised to 40 inches. Special bracing of the rear end of the frame for pintle mounting was specified, and no aluminium was to be used in the cylinder head of the motor which was required to be of at least four cylinders.[25] Since the Infantry and Cavalry had expressed a desire that eight of the trucks be of the four-wheel steer type, provision for these was also made.[26] Although a valuable military characteristic because of the great mobility and manoeuverability it lent to the jeep, the four-wheel steer feature never became standardised, principally because of the opposition of the Quartermaster Corps. Despite the wishes of the Cavalry, which wanted the four-wheel feature and later attempted to have that type standardised, the Quartermaster Corps, viewing the matter from the important standpoints of production and standardisation, saw that the four-wheel steer jeep would use four instead of two of the critical bottleneck items so essential to the all-wheel drive—the constant velocity joint[27]—and that its standardisation would mean one more maintenance problem. Thus the four-wheel steer jeep was to provide another basis for technical differences of opinion between the using arms and the supply service.

In the meantime, the American Bantam Car Company had gone ahead with the laying out of the jeep proper, in accordance with the rough sketch and general specifications arrived at between its engineers and the Ordnance subcommittee at their 19 June conference. On several occasions it was necessary for Bantam engineers to visit Holabird to iron out different engineering matters. The Spicer Manufacturing Company of Toledo, Ohio, which had devoted considerable time to the development of a four-wheel drive, was also called in by Bantam for consultation and became the axle supplier for the jeep from then on. Both the Bantam people and Holabird agreed that the standard Bantam motor would have to be stepped up in power, resulting in the development by Continental Motors Corporation of the heavier engine that was installed in the 70 original jeeps.[28]

Prepared now to undertake the construction and delivery of the 70 Bantam jeeps with four-wheel drive and 85 cubic inch motors, the American Bantam Company offered to negotiate a contract with the Quartermaster Corps for the lot at a price of $2,500 per car, making a total of $175,000 or the exact amount authorised by the War Department.[29] This the Quartermaster Corps refused to do, despite the previous recommendation of the Chief of Infantry that the negotiated procedure be followed for this development. In its letter of 10 July to the Assistant Secretary of War requesting approval for the issuance of a 10-day advertisement under the invitation for bids, the OQMG considered the Bantam offer "reasonable for such a development programme," but since the offer involved tooling costs, it felt that "acceptance would place the firm at a decided advantage over competitors in possible future procurement of this type of vehicle." While noting that the preliminary development of the jeep had been accomplished with the collaboration of the American Bantam firm, the OQMG nevertheless believed it advisable to resort to the competitive bidding procedure in order "to permit any other qualified and interested producers to submit bids." It mentioned the fact that beside the Bantam concern the Quartermaster Corps knew of only one other potential bidder.[30] While the alternative bidder was not named in this letter, it would seem clear from the foregoing that even before the initial procurement of the first 70 jeeps, the QMC had in mind the possibility of other sources for the production of the 1/4-ton. Clearance for the issuance of bids was given by the Office of the Assistant Secretary of War the following day.[31]

When the bids were opened, the competitor of the American Bantam Company was disclosed as the Willys-Overland Company of Toledo, Ohio. For some time prior to 1940, this concern had been trying to interest the Government in using some of its cars as experimental machine gun or personnel carriers. In December 1938, through their contact with the QMC Motor Procurement Planning Office at Detroit,[32] Willys-Overland offered to place one or two of their cars at the disposal of the Quartermaster Corps for test.[33] The QMC Transportation Division, in which motor transport functions were then located, informed the Detroit planning office through the OQMG, that procurement of motor vehicles in an emergency would be governed by the existing military characteristics, and that the current ones did not cover a vehicle conforming to the specifications of the Willys product. It advised further that since military characteristics were not drawn up without the objective need of a vehicle being clear, and since the Transportation Division was not aware of the objective need of any vehicle such as those made by the Willys concern, no good purpose would be served by making the suggested tests. The Willys-Overland Company continued to maintain its contact with the War Department, however, and by the first of the year succeeded in having one of its four cylinder, light five-passenger sedans tested at Fort Knox, with further tests scheduled for Fort Bragg and Fort Benning.[34] Undoubtedly appreciative of both the immediate and potential value of Government contracts, Willys now entered the lists against American Bantam on the first jeep contract. Ford, at about this time, was apparently not interested in the jeep, at least not officially, although as later events showed, it undoubtedly was keeping a close eye on developments all the time.

The technical analysis of the Bantam and Willys bids made by Holabird, revealed that while the Willys bid was nominally low, it actually was higher than Bantam's, when to it was added the liquidated damages which would result from the acknowledged inability of Willys to make delivery within the time limit of seventy-five days specified in the invitation for bids. Therefore both the Chief of the Engineering Branch and the Purchasing and Contracting Officer at Holabird recommended that the contract award be made to American Bantam Company, since "the product described in the bid submitted by the American Bantam Car Company most nearly meets the specification requirements, [and] is lowest in price . . ." The Holabird officers noted several exceptions and deviations from the specifications in the Bantam bid and suggested that the using arms be consulted on these so that all "controversial questions" could be adjusted by the time of the award. They also suggested that the specifications should be revised as soon as the results of the field tests were available. On the above basis the Office of the Quartermaster General, on 25 July 1940, awarded the contract for the 70 trucks, having a total net value of $171,185.75, to the American Bantam Company.[35]

In accordance with the agreement in its bid, the American Bantam Car Company built and delivered the first pilot model to Holabird in 49 days. During the construction of this original model, the bugaboo of weight cropped up again. It became evident to both American Bantam and Holabird that strength and material limitations, as well as other engineering factors, would make it virtually impossible to meet the 1,275 pounds weight requirement. Hence all 70 jeeps weighed some hundred pounds more, although still less than the 2,100 pound limit set in the tentative specifications of 7 July 1941, or the still later revised military characteristics of 3 July 1942, which raised the final weight of the jeep, for the period covered by this study, to not more than 2,450 pounds. The American Bantam jeep always remained the lightest of the three competitors, weighing 2,026 pounds at about the time of the Truman Committee's investigation into the jeep contracts.[36]

The Infantry viewed the increase in weight of the pilot model with disfavour. Stating that he was "gravely concerned over the tendency towards increasing weight in this vehicle," the Chief of Infantry called for the elimination of some of the excess weight in the production models "through refinements in design." Again he reiterated the position of the Infantry in respect of the jeep: that it was "in no sense a cargo vehicle but is intended for reconnaissance and liaison missions only, carrying a normal load of not to exceed three men, with one machine gun for anti-aircraft defence and a relatively small ammunition supply." Power and sturdiness adequate for cross-country work was all that was required or wanted. Additional weight, the Chief of Infantry continued, would render man-handling impracticable and would destroy its usefulness, placing it in the same general class as the ½-ton weapons carrier with the lighter field still unprovided for.

He levelled a similar criticism against any attempt to raise the low silouette and insisted that the forty-inch limit at the highest point of the jeep should under no circumstances be exceeded. In agreeing to waive, because of the urgent situation, the customary extended service test prior to adoption and to accept the Holabird tests in lieu thereof, the Chief of Infantry wanted it understood that he was not surrendering any of his normal functions in respect to the drafting of military characteristics. Therefore, if the procuring agency contemplated any essential changes from the original characteristics, the Chief of Infantry made it clear that he or his authorized representatives were to be consulted about them, and that "such equipment be not contracted for without his prior concurrence."[37] But the views of the Infantry were not to prevail. After the original pilot model had passed the severe Holabird test,[38] during which substantial changes were effected, as was the case with practically any new motor development, Bantam was ordered to proceed with the construction of the remaining 69 jeeps, all 70, according to Mr. Fenn, Bantam's president, being constructed entirely by hand.

Military Uses and Performance of the Jeep

When the jeep reached the using arms in the field its success was instant and sensational. At posts, camps and stations all over the country, it won the admiration of everyone for the manner in which it performed. The demonstrations it gave of climbing and leaping, and its all-round ability to push its way through tough situations, impressed all beholders. Neither sand, snow, nor mud seemed to hold any terrors for this quarter-ton "blitz-buggy," the tactical mission of which was to do a faster, harder-hitting job than any similar vehicle used by the renowned Nazi Panzer divisions.

Its four-wheel drive proved that it could operate over the roughest terrain. Water eighteen inches in depth was forded with ease. Although riding in the jeep was far from pleasure driving, its auxiliary transmission, providing six speeds forward and two reverse, enabled it to hit a mile-a-minute clip on the highway or claw its way up grades of 60% or better, in low. In its appearance, too, the jeep was radically different. Soon well-known to every school-boy on the street were its squat, rectangular, utilitarian shape in its coat of olive-drab, lustreless enamel that had been developed shortly before; its low silhouette; the flat fenders on each of which an additional man could be carried if necessary; the heavy brushguard protecting the front; the folding windshield and detachable folding top or canopy; the pintle and towing hooks; the heavy duty mud-and-snow tread tyres; and the front and rear blackout lights.

So versatile did the jeep prove that its uses multiplied in a fashion never even dreamed of by its creators, who thought they were merely designing a vehicle to be used by the Infantry and Field Artillery for reconnaissance purposes in forward areas and as a prime-mover for the 37mm anti-tank and anti-aircraft gun. Later, when news reports began to come in from theatres of operations all over the world—from Australia, Russia, Africa, New Guinea, Alaska and the Solomons, it was realised that the truck, ¼-ton, 4x4, had attained for itself and the Quartermaster Corps a reputation, equal in its way, perhaps, to that of the famous Flying Fortress of the Air Forces, or the General Sherman tank that was the pride of the Ordnance Department.

In these subsequent actual combat operations, the jeep which by then had reched a high stage of development, was proved successful by every arm and service. Squads of them armed with machine and anti-tank guns went into action against attacks by tanks and supporting infantry. With special equipment the jeep ran emergency telephone lines in the field and kept communications open under attack. Anti-aircraft jeeps guarded highways from enemy strafing from the air while truck convoys safely brought up supplies of essential materials. Racing "wide open" over all kinds of terrain, jeeps laid smoke screens to delay and confuse mass tank assaults by the enemy. Equipped with searchlights fed by portable generators, they wheeled into position at night to replace or reinforce fixed installations in picking enemy raiders out of the sky so that anti-aircraft batteries could shoot them down or beat them off. With medical units in this war backing up the fighting forces right on the battlefield, the jeep was used to rush precious medical supplies to doctors in the field. When allied airfields were attacked by enemy bombers, it was the jeep that was usually pressed into service to tow the grounded planes off to safety.[39] And when cables had to be laid under landing fields, it again was this little "plug-ugly" that was trundled out, hitched to a plough, a cable reel, and a roller, to do a two-day pick-and-shovel job in two hours. Photographs of the jeep in action reproduced in newspapers and other publications in the country throughout 1942-1943, showed it performing such unusual services as substituting for a switch engine overseas, with steel wheels being used instead of rubber tyres; hauling a dolly-trainload of heavy bombs, consisting of five 4-wheel trailer-dollies each loaded with approximately six large bombs, across Henderson Field at Guadalcanal to waiting Flying Fortresses and Liberators; and even being used on the deck of an aircraft carrier in the Pacific to lug torpedo bombers into take-off position for the attack against Jap-held Wake Island in October 1943.

These and many other feats of the jeep caused newspapermen accompanying allied forces, many of them driving their own jeeps, to heap praise upon it in a constant procession of jeep stories to the American public. One well-known war correspondent eulogised the jeep as follows: " . . . good Lord, I don't think we could continue the war without the jeep. It does everything. It goes everywhere. Its as faithful as a dog, as strong as a mule, and as agile as a goat. It constantly carries twice what it was designed for, and still keeps on going. It doesn't even ride so badly after you get used to it . . . the jeep is a divine instrument of wartime locomotion."[40]

While never intended for cargo duty, the jeep frequently was called upon to perform yeoman service as a supply carrier in regions where it usually was the only vehicle available or where larger trucks simply could not manoeuvre. Of the work of the jeep on the jungle trails of New Guinea, a communication from QMC officers who went through the Buna Campaign, stated: "The Jeep and the C ration . . . are two of the seven wonders of this war. There are no roads, to go through one must head for wherever there appears to be a dry stretch or where there is some likelihood of getting through. It is amazing how the jeeps keep going under such conditions. Without them, supply would have been impossible."[41]

It will be recalled that one of the requirements for the Howie Machine-Gun Carrier was that it be small enough to be lifted into a 1½-ton truck. With its dimensions of 3 feet 4 inches in height, 56 inches in width, and its length of 11 feet, the jeep not only could be lifted into a truck of this size, but it also was small enough to be flown in Army transport planes. Even before Pearl Harbour requests were being made for jeeps in commection with Airborne Task Force vehicle tests at the Aberdeen Proving Grounds, Aberdeen, Maryland,[42] and afterwards the hauling of jeeps in cargo planes was to become commonplace.

In 1942, in addition to the amphibious counterpart of the jeep then under development and which was later carried through to successful completion, to be used with notable success in the Sicilian and Italian landings in the summer and fall of 1943, tests were also ordered for the development of a conversion track suitable for installation on the jeep which would permit it to travel over deep snow and ice at a speed of at least twenty miles per hour with full pay load.[43] Should campaigns be necessary for the winter of 1943-1944, the jeep may yet be seen in this novel dress carrying on like a snow-sled in the cold regions likely to become active theatres in the present global war.

The diversified military purposes to which it was possible to put the jeep during one or two years following its development caused the Army to give consideration to the possibility of using it as a substitute for larger trucks in conjunction with the production bottleneck that developed after Pearl Harbour in the procurement of 2½-ton and heavier trucks.[44] Prior to Pearl Harbour, the jeep had alredy officially replaced the motorcycle with sidecar, and the Quartermaster General had been directed to issue jeeps to Infantry square-division regiments on a one-for-one replacement basis.[45] Partial replacement of the ½-ton command reconnaissance truck by the jeep also took place in 1941, when the jeep began to be used in posts, camps and stations all over ther country, as well as for other purposes, resulting in the QMC Motor Transport Division being advised by the arms and services that their total requirements for the ½-ton would probably be materially reduced.[46]

By 1942 the Air Corps was considering the use of three jeeps with three trailers to replace the bottleneck 2½-ton truck.[47] Substitution of the jeep for the ¾-ton in all Infantry and certain Field Artillery units also was being contemplated.[48] Around July 1942, General Marshall, Chief of Staff, sent a cablegram to theatre commanders requesting them to examine closely their requirements for tactical vehicles with the idea of using jeeps and ¾-tons in place of various larger trucks. According to the Director of Motor Transport, this plan was seen to have tremendous possibilities, not only for the standardisation of parts but also for the utilisation of the large surplus productive capacity of the automobile industry on light trucks, a capacity not then available for the 2½-ton size.[49]

Who Developed the Jeep?

While the question of who developed the jeep is not nearly so important as the fact that it *was* developed and *has* contributed mightily to the mechanised warfare of the Allies, the debate that has taken place on this subject ever since the initial success of the jeep, has served a useful purpose. The relative claims and arguments of Army protagonists and the Bantam and Willys groups have illustrated the differences in the respective functions of the Army and the automobile industry in the developent of a new motor vehicle and have underscored the fact that under the procurement and standardisation policies of the War Department, neither the Army nor the motor industry can ever be entirely independent of the other in such a development.

It has been shown thus far that an idea for a new motor vehicle about 1940-1941 could have originated anywhere; that once the idea was "sold to", or adopted by a using arm, that branch determined the proposed vehicle's military characteristics; and that specifications were then prepared by the procurement service concerned—in the case of the jeep, by the Quartermaster Corps. Because of the procurement policy then in force, motor specifications had to be general in nature in order to provide for competitive bidding, and the vehicles so procured were required to be commercial models with only such alterations as would be necessary to conform to the desired military characteristics. The purpose of this War Department policy, of course, was to assure the mass production of trucks in the event of war. At the same time, in the several years before 1940, it had been shown that this procurement policy was having a serious effect upon the Army's efforts to standardise motor vehicles into a few basic sizes and types. Ever since the need for standardisation had been forcibly demonstrated by motor transport maintenance experiences in World War I, the accomplishment of standardisation had been the goal of the Quartermaster Corps. Some grasp of past efforts made in this direction in the United States Army is essential to an understanding of the recent functional relationships between the Army and the automotive industry in the development of motor vehicles. Knowledge of the origin and evolution of War Department standardisation and procurement policy in the two decades between the first and second World Wars should also prove helpful in following the succeeding actions and events in the procurement story of the jeep contained in the next chapter.

During the First World War all of the arms and services procured their own vehicles independently, resulting in the employment of 216 makes and types. This presented an impossible maintenance problem because of inability to supply the vast munber of different spare parts required. The failure of motor maintenance in World War I made it clear that in the future a policy of standardisation of motor vehicles, based upon a minimum number of chassis types, would have to be adopted. Actually, a start towards standardisation was made in this war when the Class "B" standardised 3-5 ton truck was produced in 1917 and 1918. Not one of these trucks, however, was ever put into operation before the Armistice.

Because of the great surplus of trucks left from the war and the return of the Army to its peacetime status, few purchases of motor vehicles were made until 1929. In 1926 studies were undertaken to determine the classification of trucks required by the Army and this led to an experiment by the Quartermaster Corps on a standardised system of multiple drive trucks. By 1932 Holabird had constructed 147 trucks in four or five general weight classifications with several types of drive in each category. These trucks were assembled from standard parts and assemblies secured from the individual parts makers. While naturally pleasing to the parts manufacturers, the idea of the Army developing and assembling its own trucks was equally as displeasing to the truck manufacturers. In addition to the opposition of this group, the excessive cost of development, the difficulty of keeping abreast of rapid engineering changes in the automobile industry (funds for research and development were practically non-existent during the depression), and the lack of facilities to secure immediate mass production in the event of an emergency, were some of the factors that led to the abandonment of this experiment. On 11 September 1933, the War Department issued its General

Orders No. 9 which, in paragraph 2(a), set forth the policy that henceforth the procurement of motor vehicles would be "as complete vehicles from the automotive industry." This policy ended the QMC's venture into government manufacture of trucks of their own design. From then on, all purchased vehicles were commercial models with such modifications as to make them suitable for military use.

Therefore, when the Army embarked upon the quantity procurement of motor vehicles for the CCC in 1933 and for the PWA in 1935, little regard could be given to the question of standardisation. The extent to which dis-standardisation flourished during this period is indicated by the fact that in 1937 approximately 22 different makes and models of passenger cars and 109 makes and models of trucks were on hand with the number still increasing. Spare parts for these trucks were secured by local purchases from dealers, and while this was satisfactory for peacetime procurement as long as these trucks were in regular commercial production and large stocks of parts were available all over the country, it was realised that in the event of war, maintenance of such a diversity of trucks in theatres of operation would prove an impossible task.

For this reason, when the Secretary of War on 21 October 1936, directed that a War Department Committee be appointed to study the question of facilitating the maintenance of motor vehicles, one of the matters the committee was directed to look into was the reduction in the number of types of vehicles and the standardisation of a few basic chassis requirements to be fixed for future long-range development. In August of the following year the committee made its report to the Assistant Chief of Staff, G-4, and recommended the adoption of nine basic truck chassis types for peacetime procurement and seven for wartime. By 1939 the War Department was in a position to restate its procurement policies in official form; substantially these were the same as those later contained in Army Regulations No. 850-15 of 29 September 1939. In its memorandum to the Quartermaster General, dated 12 August 1939, the War Department standardised the all-wheel drive for tactical motor transport and limited military requirements in the general purpose tactical category to the following five chassis types: ½-ton; 1½-ton; 2½-ton; 4-ton and 7½-ton. The ¼-ton jeep was introduced in 1940, and the ¾-ton to replace the ½-ton, made its debut in 1941. A 4-5 ton, a 5-6 ton and a 6-ton chassis were also added to fill the gap between the 4 and 7½-ton groups.

In the evolution of War Department standardisation policy, besides the experiment of the Quartermaster Corps in assembling its own standardised fleet, two other possible methods of achieving standardisation were given consideration. One was to restrict purchases to those models of one commercial manufacturer in each weight classification which most closely approached military requirements; the second was to require vehicles to be assembled by the automobile industry from the standard commercial units and assemblies that also came closest to meeting requirements. Under the peacetime competitive bidding regulations, the use of the first of these methods was forbidden, although it was admitted to have great possibilities in respect to the light car and truck field. The second method was considered satisfactory for the heavier truck classifications, most of these being of the assembled type anyway. In this connection, however, the resistance of the powerful integrated-type truck manufacturers in the heavier fields had to be coped with. Nevertheless, the way to the use of both of these standardisation methods was thrown open in 1940 when the first breach was made in the mandatory use of competitive bidding methods.

In July of that year, Congress authorised war contracting "with or without advertising." The Office of the Secretary of War immediately followed this up with a directive permitting awards to be made without formal competitive bidding whenever such methods "will serve to expedite the accomplishment of the defence program." These and other actions now made possible the negotiation of contracts, and, as a result, a combination of both of the approved plans for achieving standardisation began to be put into effect. In the heavier field, the 6-ton prime mover was to be made of standard major units by the White, Federal and Autocar companies. For the medium types, Chevrolet and Yellow Truck and Coach, both divisions of General Motors, were first selected to make exclusively their 1½-ton truck and 2½-ton truck, respectively. In the lighter field, the outstanding example of identical construction was to be the jeep, which ultimately was to be made by both Ford and Willys from the designs and blueprints of the Willys model.[50]

From all of the foregoing, it should be clear why the Army since 1933 has never completely designed or engineered any of its motor vehicles. The only exception was the one Howie Machine-Gun Carrier designed and built by Captain R.G. Howie for experimental purposes. Even in this vehicle, Captain Howie made use of standard automobile and motorcycle parts. Precluded by regulations from designing and building its own trucks, the Army's functions in the development of any new motor vehicle technically ended with the preparation of the military characteristics by the using arms and the writing of the specifications by the Quartermaster Corps. The automotive engineers of private industry carried on from that point and generally designed, engineered, and built the model in accordance with the stated specifications. The development of a motor vehicle for military purposes therefore had to be somewhat in the nature of a dual enterprise, an attempt to obtain a meeting of minds between the Army, which set forth the characteristics and specifications, and the automobile industry, which translated them into an acceptable motor vehicle. Patently, collaboration and consultation on all aspects of the development, including design and engineering, had to take place constantly between the two if the undertaking was to be crowned with success.

The development of the ¼-ton was no exception to the above procedure. In speaking of the evolution of the jeep the Quartermaster General himself said: "It is a matter of common sense that industry can neither design nor supply the Army's needs if it does not know them. At the same time, the Army should not attempt to dictate engineering details except insofar as military needs differ from general practice in the industry, or where experience shows normal standards to be inadequate."[51] The account presented in the preceding pages of this study indicates that this is precisely what happened in the case of the ¼-ton, and it would seem that the Army and the American Bantam Company therefore must share honours for its development. The dispute thus boils down to the somewhat academic question of deciding who did most of the work and who should get most of the credit. Since this was a matter of opinion as well as fact, the evidence advanced by the different groups and persons concerned is often contradictory.

We have seen that the using arms for a long while had been interested in both a substitute for the motorcycle with sidecar for command-reconnaissance purposes and the development of a light weapons carrier. For the period 1937-1940, it appeared that the only commercial car on the market that came close to meeting these requirements was the product of the American Bantam Company. Apparently, neither Ford nor Willys had anything comparable to it at the time. Realising the potentialities of its car for Army use, the Bantam people were aggressive in calling attention to its merits to any military personnel that would listen. They found an attentive ear in the Infantry and other using arms, but claimed that other quarters of the War Department were rather apathetic to the idea, regarding the Bantam vehicle as little more than a toy and curiosity with no real military usefulness. The American Bantam Company stated that it was not until the initiation of the matter by the Secretary of War through the General Staff that the Quartermaster Corps was induced to consider the Bantam car.[52] In its general investigation of the national defence programme, the House Military Affairs Committee had this to say of the origin of the jeep:

> American Bantam Car Co., according to reports, had originated the idea of producing these cars for the War Department and about two years earlier at the expense of the company, had a representative in Europe survey all cars of this character being used by various armies; that thereafter that company brought it to the attention of the War Department, endeavouring to have them introduce these cars but it was not until they reached the Secretary of War himself that they succeeded in getting any action. Colonel Hester has stated that they are of tremendous value.[53]

Testifying before the Truman Committee, which also investigated the reasons why the Bantam concern later was excluded from a share in the jeep contracts, Francis H. Fenn, Bantam's President, was queried by Senator Mead on the creation of the jeep as follows:

> *Senator Mead.* And is it true that you pioneered and developed this idea of the small car?
> *Mr. Fenn.* It is most emphatically true, sir. It is so true that I personally saw Ford Motor Co. representatives in under our car in a grease pit at Holabird with a clip board making freehand drawings of the lay-out.
> *Senator Mead.* Then you really got the first educational order?
> *Mr. Fenn.* We had the first car down there, the first car to be tested, and it was looked over by the other two manufacturers from stem to stern, without any question, or any interference, or anything else.[54]

23

Lt. Col. Edwin Van Deusen represented the Quartermaster Corps at this investigation and when it came his turn to give testimony the Chairman of the Committee questioned him as to the "Army's attitude and the history of this thing as far as the Army is concerned." Confirming the first witness' testimony, Colonel Van Deusen replied: "The history of the development of the truck is substantially as outlined by Mr. Fenn."[55]

Other Army spokesmen, both officially and semi-officially, have expressed quite opposite views. In an article on the jeep written for the *Quartermaster Review*, the Motor Transport public relations officer stated: "Credit for the original design of the Army's truck ¼-ton, 4x4, may not be claimed by any single individual or any single manufacturer. This vehicle is the result of much research and many tests. Army engineers, both military and civilian, at the Holabird Quartermaster Depot did the bulk of work in designing it."[56] Similarly, in the second endorsement of the Quartermaster General sharply protesting the decision of the General Staff to procure the first 1,500 production jeeps from the Bantam Company, after the completion of the original seventy, the Bantam jeep was not considered a pilot model but rather "a preliminary engineering model, most of the parts of which were made in the tool room and which represents an assembled vehicle designed primarily by the engineers of the Holabird Quartermaster Depot, the unit manufacturers and the engineer of the Bantam Company; for example, the present body design was based almost entirely on drawings furnished by Holabird and the axles and transfer case were designed by the Spicer Mfg. Corporation."[57] A follow-up memorandum to the Deputy Chief of Staff objecting to the overruling decision of the General Staff on the Quartermaster General's preceding second endorsement, substantially reiterated the above statement and added further that "not a single unit of the original Bantam is in the present vehicle, nor is a single major unit of the present vehicle produced by the Bantam Company itself."[58]

The argument was further complicated later on when the procurement fight ended with the Willys model chosen for standardisation and mass production by both that concern and Ford. Willys lost little time in initiating a nation-wide advertising campaign through newspapers, magazines and radio broadcasts setting forth its connection with the development of the jeep. The following extract from one of the advertisements, taken from a popular national weekly, was a typical example: "The Jeep calls them Daddy . . . . The Quartermaster Corps of the U.S. Army and the Civilian Engineers of Willys-Overland." The text then continued on the theme "These are the men [the Willys engineers] whose engineering skill and creative minds, added to those of the Quartermaster Corps of the US Army, gave birth to the amazing Jeep of today."[59] Another advertisement, picturing the jeeps in action under fire and alliteratively referring to them as "motorized mustangs of our modern mobile army—Willys-built Jeeps," went on to say: "It was the great Willys civilian engineering staff fresh from their triumphs in the Willys-Americar and Go-Devil engine, who collaborated with the Quartermaster Corps of the US Army to create and perfect the jubilant jeep."[60]

Because of these and many other similar advertising claims made by the Willys Company, the US Federal Trade Commission issued a complaint against it, charging it with misrepresentation in advertising. The Commission charged that Willys did not "create and perfect the 'Jeep', nor was it "the designer or the sole manufacturer" of it, as current Willys advertisements claimed. "In truth and in fact," said the Commission, "the idea of creating the Jeep was originated by the American Bantam Car Company of Butler, Pennsylvania, in collaboration with certain officers of the United States Army, and the same was developed by the American Bantam Car Company in collaboration with said officers, and not by the respondent, Willys-Overland Motors, Inc."[61]

At least one of the using arms of the Army, the Infantry apparently regarded neither Willys nor Ford as having anything to do with the jeep's creation, for in a letter dealing with comparative tests of all three jeeps, made by the Infantry Board, the Chief of Infantry once wrote: "The Ford and Willys-Overland models are copies of the original Bantam design. . ."[62]

With the foregoing facts—and opinions—on the issue of who developed the jeep, in his possession, it is left to the reader to draw his own conclusions.

NOTES to CHAPTER I

1   The Austin was the American edition of the well-known baby Austin manufactured in England. Licence to manufacture this car in the United States was issued to the American Austin Company of Butler, Pennsylvania in 1929. In 1936 this company was taken over by a new concern and became the American Bantam Car Company, builder of the first successful models of the jeep.

      The small, light car, extremely popular in Europe because of the high cost of fuel and heavy taxes on cars with large motors, never did become well-liked by the American motorist, to whom the cost of gasoline was not as great and who preferred a larger, more powerful automobile better suited to the greater driving ranges and more varied operating conditions of this country. The phenomenal success of the jeep, however, may cause a new wave of popularity for the small car in this country after the present war is over.

2   QM 400.112 (Automobiles) Austin, IB 451, Infantry Board to Chief of Infantry, 8 November 1932, "Austin Car for Test", with succeeding endorsements.

3   The price of this one little car for which there were "no funds available", originally was quoted by the local dealer to the Quartermaster as $262.25, less freight and dealer's discount. Less than a decade later the QMC Motor Transport Division's appropriations for the purchase of motor vehicles alone, for the fiscal years 1940-1942, were more than a billion and a half dollars, covering requirements for over 1,000,000 vehicles of all kinds. Appropriation Report, QMC Motor Transport Planning Branch, 13 April 1942; Survey of Army Supply Program, MT Service, QMC, 8 May 1942; OQMG Annual Report, 1942.

4   Captain Wendell G. Johnson, Infantry, "The Howie Machine-Gun Carrier", *Infantry Journal*, November-December 1937, pp 529-531.

5   *Ibid*; US Army Tentative Specifications, USA-LP-91-997A, 7 July 1941.

6   *Ibid*

7   *Ibid*

8   The Motor Transport Division was given separate divisional status by OQMG Office Order No. 49, 26 July 1940. Prior to that time it had been a branch (along with the Water Transport and Commercial Traffic branches) of the QMC Transportation Division, organisation and functions of which were set forth in Office Order No. 4, 7 January 1937.

9   When the Army was reorganised on 2 March 1942, by WD Circular No. 59, resulting in the separation of the supply functions of the General Staff into a separate Services of Supply, the review and approval of development requests were vested in the requirements Division of the latter organisation. The name of the Services of Supply was later changed to the Army Service Forces.

10   Army Regulations No. 850-15, 29 September 1939. On 1 August 1942, all functions relating to the two types of vehicles were consolidated under one organisation by the transfer of the entire QMC Motor Transport Service to the Ordnance Department. WD Circular No. 245, 25 July 1942. While none of the official directives relating to the transfer specifically state why it was made, among the several possible reasons for it, the elimination of duplication of functions probably was the most important. This was especially true of the two almost parallel sets of maintenance installations that had come to be established by both agencies.

11 Official delegations of Army trucks indicate the number of driving wheels. Thus a "4x4" means "four wheels and four wheel driving," a "6x6" shows "six wheels driving," etc.

12 Descriptions of the development, testing, and procurement processes of military motor vehicles may be found in Capt. J.E. Engler's "Procurement and Testing Military Motor Vehicles," on file in the OQMG Historical Section; pertinent extracts from this paper are in the *SAE Journal*, v. 49, no. 1, July 1941. See also Major E.H. Holtzkemper, QMC, "Engineering Branch Motor Transport Service", *Quartermaster Review* May-June 1942.

13 "Minutes of the QMC Technical Committee," 18 November 1938, including 2nd and 6th endorsements from the Secretary of War, 17 and 21 December 1938, respectively.

14 The ½-ton truck was not entirely replaced by the later jeep. However, when the tremendous success of the ¼-ton became assured in 1940 and 1941, a new ¾-ton truck, modelled along the lines of the jeep, was developed and the ½-ton was discontinued. The military characteristics of the ¾-ton were first laid down by MCM No. 12, 7 November 1941. Up to July 1942, the jeep and its ¾-ton big brother remained the only two distinct departures from commercial design in the Army's category of general-purpose, tactical motor vehicles.

15 QM 400.112 (Vehicle Motor Light), CI 470.8/550 XII "C", Chief of Infantry to Adjutant General, "Light Vehicle Development," 6 June 1940.

16 *Ibid*, 1st endorsement, 8 June 1940.

17 *Ibid*, 2nd endorsement, 14 June 1940.

18 *Ibid*, 3rd endorsement, 14 June 1940. In 1938 the American Bantam Company sold the Quartermaster Corps three chassis for experimental purposes, but they did not prove successful. As a result, when in September of the following year American Bantam offered additional units to the Quartermaster Corps for further tests, they were informed "that there appeared no further military requirements for that type of vehicle that they built." About February 1940, Mr. Charles H. Payne was employed by the Bantam concern to represent it in Washington on the sale of its products to the Government; as a result of his efforts there were developed in the using arms and services the requirements for a light, low car approaching the Bantam product. Testimony of Francis H. Fenn, President, American Bantam Car Company, Butler, Pennsylvania, in *Hearings Before a Special Committee Investigating the National Defense Program, US Senate, 77th Congress*, Part 7, 6 August 1941; Testimony of Lt. Colonel Edwin S. Van Deusen, QMC, Chief, Procurement Branch, Motor Transport Division, *ibid*. Herafter referred to as *Truman Committee Hearings*.

19 An official statement by Colonel Howie in 1943, of his connection with the development of the jeep, states that his machine, in addition to tests by the Infantry Board in 1937 that evoked favourable comment and recommendation for further development, had also been tested by the Second Division under the command of Major General Walter Krueger, at Fort Sam Houston. General Krueger's report was to the effect that the Howie Carrier filled the need for a vehicle of that type. During 1938 and 1939, Howie demonstrated the carrier to both military personnel and civilians, including Bernard Baruch. Used by the 29th Infantry for several months in tests and manoeuvres, Howie said that by 1940 the carrier had gone over 4,000 miles, most of it cross-country, and that its practical usefulness had been demonstrated. Colonel R.G. Howie to TAG, "Certificate re history of development of ¼-ton truck," 23 June 1943. For text of Colonel Howie's entire statement, see Appendix.

20 QM 400.112 (Vehicle Motor Light), The Adjutant General to Chief of Ordnance, 15 June 1940.

21 *Ibid,* Subcommittee on Automotive Equipment to The Ordnance Committee, Technical Staff, "Light Infantry and Cavalry Vehicles," 22 June 1940.

22 *Ibid,* Major Howie remained at the Bantam plant approximately seven days. The part he played in connection with the proposed development is best recounted in his own words:

> In June 1940, while I was on manoeuvres with the Provisional Tank Brigade in Louisiana, I received a radiogram from the Chief of Infantry directing me to proceed to Butler, Pennsylvania, to the Bantam Motor Car Company and to bring with me the drawings of the "Howie Carrier". Upon arrival at Butler, I met an Infantry, Ordnance and Quartermaster Committee, who informed me that 70 vehicles were to be contracted for and that I was to turn over my drawings and remain with the Bantam Company to formulate plans and specifications for the new vehicle. This vehicle was to be based on the characteristics and engineering data of the "Howie Carrier", incorporating four-wheel drive, with a capacity of three passengers. The Board also asked me to form an opinion as to whether or not the Bantam Company was capable of building the vehicle if awarded a contract. At that time the plant was not operating.
>
> The Board remained at Butler one day. During the day the plant was inspected and conferences held with Mr. Fenn, President, Mr. Payne, who was interested in negotiating the contract with the War Department, and Mr. Probst, the Chief Engineer. Before leaving Butler that night the Board directed me to remain at the Bantam Plant as long as necessary to complete plans and specifications so that the Bantam Company could proceed if and when directed. Mr. Robert F. Brown, civilian engineer, Holabird Quartermaster Depot, a member of the Board (now with Development Branch TAC) remained with me for approximately two days, during which time we discussed engineering features of the vehicle. I remained at the plant for approximately seven additional days, during which time I turned over drawings, photos and other data of the Howie carrier to the Bantam Company, wrote and submitted specifications for the new vehicle. During this period it was the desire of the Bantam Company to use many of their standard production parts and unit assemblies, without change. It was not without some discussion that I was able to convince them that the vehicle must be engineered completely as a new vehicle, and that the success of the job depended upon the inclusion of those characteristics, such as floatation, power to weight ratio, angles of approach and departure, size of axles, wheels, tyres, frame, wheelbase, tread, and power transmission, all in proper relation to each other, as were proven in the Howie carrier and which gave it cross country agility and stamina. These characteristics were incorporated into the specifications. During this period an engineer of the Spicer Corporation was called in, and a drawing of a front wheel drive, prepared by me with the aid of Mr. Albrecht . . . was given him.
>
> In July 1940, I was transferred to Fort Knox, Kentucky, as executive officer, Armored Force School, which detail precluded further participation in the production. *For Colonel Howie's complete statement, see Appendix.*

23 QM 400.112 (Vehicle, Motor Light), Subcommittee on Automotive Equipment to The Ordnance Committee, Technical Staff, "Light Infantry and Cavalry Vehicles", 22 June 1940.

24 *Ibid,* 4th endorsement, AG 451 (6/15-40), AGO to Chief of Ordnance and the Quartermaster General, in turn, 5 July 1940.

25 QM 451 (398-41-9), Tentative Specifications, Truck, Motor Gasoline, Light Reconnaissance & Command Car (Four Wheels - Four Wheel Drive), 2 July 1940.

26 QM 400.12 (Vehicle, Motor Light), Chief of Infantry to TAG, "Light Vehicle Development", (6 June 1940), 4th endorsement, Holabird to QMG, 3 July 1940.

27 Constant velocity joints are the devices on tactical all-wheel vehicles through which power is transmitted to the front wheels so as to permit them to turn to the necessary angle for steering. For the complete story of the four-wheel steer jeep, see *infra*, Chapter 3.

28 *Truman Committee Hearings*, Testimony of Francis H. Fenn, President, American Bantam Company, 6 August 1941.

29 QM 400.112 (Vehicle, Motor Light), Charles H. Payne, American Bantam Car Company to Colonel J.N. Johnson, OQMG, 9 July 1940.

30 QM 451 (398-41-9), Current Procurement Branch to ASW, "Procurement of Trucks, Light Reconnaissance and Command Cars, ¼-ton, 4x4", 10 July 1940. While the alternative bidder was not named in this letter, it would seem clear from the foregoing that even before the initial procurement of the first 70 jeeps, the QMC had in mind the possibility of other sources for the production of the ¼-ton.

31 *Ibid*, 4th endorsement, ASW to QMG, 11 July 1940.

32 Procurement Planning was a general programme of planning for war procurement and production in advance of a national emergency. It was carried on for twenty years prior to 1940 under the direct supervision of the Assistant Secretary of War, and was participated in by all of the Army supply services. In the Quartermaster Corps, a separate office for motors was maintained at Detroit. Because of the policy, laid down from the very beginning by the ASW, of complete separation of procurement planning from the operations of current procurement, there was no direct co-ordination of work between the motor planning office at Detroit and the current procurement unit at Holabird, except as effected through the OQMG at Washington. However, procurement planning on motors, because of the extensive liaison it developed between the Army and the automotive industry, particularly in respect to keep Detroit informed as to what the Army's possible requirements would be in the event of an emergency, played an important part in readying the industry for the tremendous truck production it was able to put out almost from the start. For an overall survey of the entire planning programme in the QMC, see Thomas M. Pitkin and Herbert R. Rifkind, *Procurement Planning in the Quartermaster Corps, 1920-1940*.

33 QM 095 (Willys-Overland Motors Inc.), Vol. 1, Detroit QMC Motor Planning Office to the QMG, 2nd endorsement, 28 December 1938.

34 *Ibid*, Transportation Division to War Planning and Procurement, "Allocation of Facilities, Willys-Overland Motors, Inc.," 7 January 1939; letter, ASW to Willys-Overland, 20 February 1940.

35 QM 451 (Proc. 398-41-9), Holabird to the QMG, "Invitation for Bids No. 398-41-9", 24 July 1940, including Technical Analysis; *ibid*, 1st endorsement, OQMG to Holabird, 25 July 1940; *ibid*, OQMG to Commissioner Knudson, "Contract with American Bantam", 30 July 1940. The unit price of the 62 two-wheel steer jeeps was $2,399.40 and the 8 four-wheel steer, $2,802.83. Naturally, these "development" prices were considerably higher than the later contract prices of jeep. By April 1942, the cost of the jeep was approximately $855. QM 451 M-E (Ordnance), QMG to Ordnance, "Patrol Cars", 28 April 1942.

36 *Truman Committee Hearings*, Testimony of Francis H. Fenn and Lt. Col. Edwin S. Van Deusen, 6 August 1941.

37 QM 400.112 (Vehicles, Motor Light), CI 470.8/550 XII "C", Chief of Infantry to the QMG, "Light Vehicle Development", 23 October 1940.

38   The Holabird Test Course was famous as an Army "torture test" where trucks were subjected to extreme punishment in order to prove their fitness as military vehicles. In the words of one writer it practically amounted "to rolling it [the truck] down the Grand Canyon", or as another Motor Transport officer put it, "that test course tortures a truck like an inquisitional rack, and if a truck has anything to confess, it confesses." In general, the testing procedure was as follows:

Upon arrival at Holabird the pilot model was given a laboratory technical and engineering inspection including the checking of dimensions, general construction, ground and wheel clearances, angles of approach and departure, cooling ability, driver visibility, etc. Dynamometer tests were also made. Next followed a field test in which the vehicle was tried to the utmost. It included 5,000 miles of normal highway operation with full payloads and towed loads. Then, under the same load conditions, a 1,000 mile cross-country test had to be undergone. This was a severe trial that included going through mud holes, up hills with grades of 65%, over large ditches, and around small twisting hills that frequently caused frame distortion; maximum speeds during this ordeal averaged but seven to nine miles per hour. After this, another 1,000 miles was run on a concentrated section of clay road, followed by 500 more miles on a rolling sand course under full pay and towed load. Finally there came the last ten hours of operation up a sand grade of such slope that the vehicles was forced to travel in its lowest gear at about $1\frac{1}{2}$ to 2 miles an hour. During all of these tests frames generally bent and cracked, springs broke, bearings burned out, transmissions had to be replaced and many other failures occurred. If caused by faulty design or material, these had to be corrected before the vehicle was considered acceptable.

With the completion of the operations trials, which jammed perhaps 50,000 miles of normal vehicle life into the few thousand miles of the concentrated test, the pilot model was torn down and all of the parts minutely inspected for wear and fractures, all of which was embodied in the full and exact report made to the manufacturer. A conference was then held by the various Army and factory engineers engaged in the test. Defects to be eliminated and changes to be made were agreed upon, and only when satisfactory solutions had been submitted by the maker, was he notified to proceed with production. At the factory a Government inspector checked each vehicle carefully as it came off the assembly line.

When a sufficient number of the development vehicles had been distributed to the various using arms in the field, their own boards went to work on their own tests and reports. These were finally co-ordinated with the Holabird reports and the whole reviewed by the Quartermaster Technical Committee which decided upon the suitability of the truck for military use. If acceptable, the military characteristics and specifications were revised wherever necessary, and the vehicle was then ready for quantity production. Capt. J.E. Engler, QMC, "Procurement and Testing Military Motor Vehicles", delivered before the SAE, July 1941; Address by Colonel E.S. Van Deusen, before the Metropolitan Chapter, SAE, New York City, February 1942. For comparative field tests between the Bantam, Ford, and Willys jeeps, see *infra*, page

39   For graphic representations of the above, see the colourful action drawings of I.B. Hazelton, reproduced in Willys-Overland advertisements (*New York Times Magazine*, 19 April 1942), approved by the War Department. Later testing by the Air Forces, the QMC Motor Transport Service, and the manufacturers, disclosed that the jeep, although its approved military characteristics and specifications limited its towed load to 1,000 pounds, could tow bombardment planes up to 20,000 pounds on hard surface. Several hundred pounds of dead weight, usually in the form of sandbags, had to be added to give the necessary extra traction, especially on soft ground or wet sod. According to the British Purchasing Commission, even tractors of the wheel type had not proved satisfactory for towing planes. The jeep, however, when tested on concrete by one of its makers, showed a draw bar pull of 1,400 pounds at the pintle hook, with an 800 pounds load, all with no undue strain on the clutch or other driving components. QM 451.2 (Trucks, ¼-ton. 4x4), "Use of Trucks, ¼-ton, 4x4, for Towing of Airplanes", 6, 13, 26 June, 11, 13, 16, 21 July 1942.

40 Ernie Pyle, *Washington Daily News*, 4 June 1943. The jeep, of course, was only one unit of the generally excellent American motor transport equipment in North Africa. The larger trucks, especially the 2½-ton model which hauled big loads and stood up under terrific punishment, also came in for their share of praise. According to reports of supply specialists returning from the North African theatres, "American motor vehicles proved vastly superior". Statement by Col. James B. Edmonds, "War Bulletins", OQMG General Service Branch, 17 June 1943.

41 Extracts from letters from Col. D.C. Cordiner, Col. J.H. Burgheim, and Capt. Charles W. Florance, Jr., OQMG Memorandum, 15 March 1943.

42 QM 400.12 M-ES (Vehicles Airborne Task Force), 19 August 1941.

43 *Ibid*, (Tracks Conversion) (EDT 76-42), 5 March 1942.

44 When war broke out for the United States, the peacetime truck industry of this country was ill-prepared to meet the tremendous impact of medium and heavy duty military truck replacement. Of the total 1939 commercial production of some 700,000 trucks, only 7% represented production capacity for vehicles of two tons or heavier, 93% being for trucks of the lighter weights. The urgent military needs upset this proportion completely by requiring 47% in the heavy classifications, or eleven times the number of such trucks produced in peacetime. Of the close to 3,000,000 trucks required by the Army for the years 1942-1943 plus six months of 1944, well over a million were in the 2-ton or heavier bracket. (To visualise this tremendous volume of truck production, one need only recall that on 1 July 1940, there were but 29,867 motor vehicles of all kinds on hand in the Army.) While light truck output, as increased from 1940 on, was more than adequate to meet those requirements, heavier truck production, despite expansion of several hundred per cent, was still far short of the Army's needs. This meant that substitute uses for the surplus of light trucks the automotive industry was able to produce had to be found, if possible, until such time as the heavier truck production could catch up and total production became balanced. "Survey of Army Supply Program", QMC Motor Transport Service, 8 May 1942.

45 QM 451 (Proc. 398-41-9), AG 451 (4-12-41) M-D, AG to QMG, "Additional Procurement of ¼-ton Trucks", 1 May 1941. QM 451 M-O, MT Operations Branch to MT Plans and Training Branch, "Motorcycles w/sidecar replaced with trucks, ¼-ton, 4x4", 19 August 1941.

46 OQMG "Daily Activity Report", 21 August 1941; QM 451. M-O, Chief, Operations Branch to Chief, Motor Transport Division, "Memorandum from USW regarding ¼-ton, 4x4, trucks", 21 October 1941.

47 QMC Motor Transport "Policy Committee Minutes", 8 May 1942.

48 *Ibid*, 8 June 1942.

49 OQMG "Weekly Progress Report" 30 June - 8 July 1942. By the end of 1943, the Willys Company was reporting that the jeep performed "at least twenty four separate tasks in the armed forces." Report in *The New York Times*, 10 December 1943.

50 QM 451 (Maintenance), January-December 1938; AG 451 (6-15-39) Misc. D., AG to QMG, "Standardization of Motor Vehicles", 21 August 1939, in Minutes of the QMC Technical Committee, 6 November 1939; Army Regulations No. 850-15, 29 September 1939; Standardisation data from Motor Transport Historical Files, OQMG Historical Section; Public Law No. 703, 76th Congress, approved 2 July 1940, Sec. 1(a); QM 400.13 (Without Advertising), SW to Chiefs of Supply Arms and Services, "Procurement without Advertising", 2 July 1940.

51   Motor Transportation in the National Defense Program", an address by Major General E.B. Gregory, Quartermaster General, to the SAE, Detroit, Michigan, 7 January 1941.

52   QM 451 (Proc. 398-41-9), Letter of Charles H. Payne, Asst. to President, American Bantam Car Company, to the Hon. Henry L. Stimson, Secretary of War, 14 October 1940; Letter of F.H. Fenn, President, American Bantam Car Company, to General Brehon B. Somervell, Services of Supply, 23 March 1942, in MT Historical Files, Historical Section, OQMG.

53   *Investigation of the National Defense Program, Interim General Report of the House Military Affairs Committee, 23 June 1942*, pages 286, 287.

54   *Truman Committee Hearings*, Testimony of Francis H. Fenn, President, American Bantam, 6 August 1941.

55   *Ibid*, Testimony of Lt. Col. Edwin S. Van Deusen, Chief, Procurement Branch, Motor Transport Division, QMC 6 August 1941.

56   Lt. E.P. Hogan, QMC, "The Story of the Quarter-Ton", *Quartermaster Review*, September-October 1941. See also Col. R.G. Howie's statement of his connection with the Bantam development, *supra*, in Chapter I. For complete text of this statement, see Appendix.

57   QM 451 (M-P) (398-41-9), QMG to AG, "Procurement of Fifteen Hundred (1,500) Trucks, ¼-ton (4x4) Light Command-Reconnaissance Trucks", 2nd endorsement, 1 November 1940. The Bantam jeep was entirely an assembled vehicle whereas the Ford and Willys models were of the type of construction termed "integrated". It is somewhat of a fallacy, however, to regard this latter type as being built from the ground up by the manufacturer making it. This is especially true of the truck field, even in the case of the so-called giants of the industry such as General Motors, makers of the 1½ and 2½-ton trucks for the Army, or Chrysler, which through its Fargo subsidiary made the Army's ½-ton and later, the ¾-ton truck. The automobile industry was based almost entirely upon the subcontracting principle and practically all truck manufacturers bought most of their parts and unit assemblies. For example, on the QMC 2½-ton made by the Yellow Truck and Coach division, of twenty-five major items in the vehicle, only four (engine, brakes, propellor shaft, and cab for body) were listed in Motor Transport tables as being their "own", and on one of these, the propellor shaft, the outside source of Spicer was also given. The Chrysler-Fargo ½-ton, a modification of the commercial Dodge truck, used its own engine, brakes, transmission, transfer case, cab, and fenders. Front and rear axles were shown as their own, except that the housings were made by Clark. In both cases, all other major components and unit assemblies came from subcontracting sources.

In the case of the jeep, the differences perhaps were even less. Ford made its own motor—adapted from the 4-cylinder Ford tractor engine—and also made its own transmission. Willys used its regular "Go-Devil" engine from its "Americar", which it assembled from parts and units procured elsewhere. The Bantam motor, on the other hand, was supplied complete by Continental. In other respects, Willys and Ford bought their parts just as Bantam did. All three jeep makers purchased their bodies, frames, wheels, axles, transfer cases, propeller shafts, universal joints, clutches, radiators, electrical equipment, and other accessory units including carburettors, fuel and oil filters, and radio suppression equipment. In some instances they received these from identical sources. For example, all three bought their frames from the Midland Steel Company and their wheels from the Kelsey-Hayes Company. The principal bottleneck item of axles, together with the constant velocity joint, propellor shaft, and transfer case, was supplied originally by only one firm—Spicer—the only source available. Bantam and Willys both used Electric-Autolite ignition equipment, Warner transmissions, and Jamestown radiator cores. The AC fuel filter was employed by both Ford and Willys; Bantam and Ford each used Long clutches. For tables on sources for GMC and Fargo major items, see draft report of Lt. Col. Douglas Dow, Motor Transport Division, QMC, in OQMG Historical Section; for data on jeep items see QM 161, American Bantam Car Company, Letter to Chief, Purchasing and Contracting Branch, Motor Transport Division, 24 July 1941; QM 161, Willys-Overland Motors, Inc., Letter to General Barzynski, Asst. QMG, 24 July 1941; QM 451 (Proc. 398-42-Neg-1) "16,000 Trucks, ¼-ton 4x4 W-398-qm-10757", Letter to Chief, Purchasing & Contracting Branch, Motor Transport Division, from Ford Motor Co., 24 July 1941.

58 QM 451 (M-P)(Proc. 398-41-9), Memorandum from QMG to General R.C. Moore, Deputy Chief of Staff, 6 November 1940.

59 Willys-Overland advertisement in *Collier's*. 11 April 1942.

60 Federal Trade Commission Docket No. 4959, 6 May 1943.

61 *Ibid.*

62 QM 400.112 (Truck, ¼-ton, 4x4), CI 451.4/9615, Chief of Infantry (through E.W. Fales, Colonel, Infantry Executive) to the President, Infantry Board re Tests of ¼-ton Trucks, Ford and Overland, 15 May 1941.

CHAPTER II

Procurement of the Jeep—The Fight for Contracts

Purchase of the First 4,500 Jeeps—1,500 each from Bantam, Ford, and Willys

By October 1940, the success of the Bantam pilot model's tests which were then well on the way to completion, had focused the attention of Ford and Willys companies on the jeep and thus set the scene for the year-long struggle for contracts that was to ensue between the three competitors. In this competition there was a wide disparity between the financial and industrial weapons with which the contestants were armed. Bantam, the smallest of the trio, with an approximate investment of one million dollars and employing around 450 men[1], was in fact a midget compared to the Ford empire with its more than one hundred thousand workers and hundreds of millions of dollars investments. Willys, about a $50,000,000 concern[2], occupied the ground between Bantam and Ford.

Both Bantam and Willys had previously been through financial difficulties and under receiverships, and both had applied to the Reconstruction Finance Corporation for first-mortgage loans, dating back to 1938 for Bantam and 1939 for Willys. The RFC had come to the rescue of both of these concerns, and it was the Government's money that enabled them to finance their jeep contracts[3]. Needless to say, this was not true of Ford.

Ford, it will be recalled, had not bid at all on the first seventy jeeps, although it had been sent an invitation to do so. Willys had bid, but its bid had been rejected because it did not meet the requirements in respect to delivery. Neither Ford nor Willys at this time had developed a vehicle that could meet the specifications for the jeep. Bantam, having the initial advantage of its regular small car as a foundation plus the additional development work it accomplished in collaboration with the Ordnance subcommittee and Holabird engineers, had submitted the only complete bid and hence had been awarded the contract.

Now, however, it became apparent that Ford and Willys were about to drive entering wedges for themselves into the jeep business. Their desire to share in the jeep contracts was endorsed by the Quartermaster Corps, which invited them to participate in a further development and production programme planned for the jeep. Representatives of the two concerns were "called in and encouraged to make major expenditures for engineering development work . . ."[4] and, in fact, already "had gone to considerable preliminary work toward production of pilot models"[5]. Insofar as revealed by the records available, the plans of the Quartermaster Corps for additional development of the jeep by Ford and Willys were first officially put into concrete form when the Motor Transport Subcommittee met on 18 October, 1940, and recommended the procurement of 500 each from the Bantam, Ford and Willys companies[6].

A few days prior to that meeting American Bantam, having learned of the QMC's intentions to bring Ford and Willys into the programme, had sent to the Secretary of War the first of the series of protests it was to make before its final elimination from the jeep programme in the following year. Expressing surprise that the Quartermaster Corps was considering the ordering of jeeps from Ford and Willys in addition to itself, Bantam reviewed the whole history of the 1/4-ton up to then and requested reconsideration of the contemplated splitting of contracts. It was claimed that Bantam had developed the jeep for the Army, in spite of early scepticism in certain quarters of the War Department, with no other automobile manufacturer contributing one iota to its successful completion". The enthusiasm of the Army over the performance of this Bantam development could be easily verified, the letter said. Further, while Bantam had devoted its entire time and engineering facilities to bringing out the jeep, practically stopping all commercial business for this purpose, Ford and Willys had continud their regular commercial production and were also developing aircraft motors, accessories, and other products.

Contending that it had more knowledge of the small-car field than anyone else, Bantam stated that its production facilities were more than sufficient to meet all Army requirements, provided the axle bottleneck was cleared up. Since this bottleneck did exist, no advantage in delivery to the Army would be gained even if the contracts were split between ten manufacturers, until the delivery of axles from Spicer, the sole source of supply, could be expedited. Should the time ever arrive when Bantam was not able to fill all Army demands it, of course, would be "glad and willing to turn over all detail drawings and other help to other automobile manufacturers in the interest of National Defence." The letter recalled that Bantam had been the only firm to submit a complete bid on the first seventy jeeps and claimed that its prices were still lower than anyone else's. Bantam had made good through "diligent, hard work and faith in our vision," and felt wholeheartedly that "until we have been given orders to our full capacity there should be no reason for your Department to search elsewhere for production."[7]

While this letter was in the hands of the Secretary of War, the report of the Motor Transport subcommittee meeting of 18 October was transmitted by the Quartermaster General to the Adjutant General. Judging from the published proceedings of the meeting, the conclusions and recommendations of the subcommittee set forth in this report had not been reached without considerable discussion between the using arms' representatives and the Quartermaster Corps.

At that conference, the majority of the committee came to the conclusion that the pilot model test of the jeep "has clearly indicated the suitability of a vehicle of this general type for military use", and that in order to expedite further the development of the jeep for which there was an urgent need, a greater quantity should be purchased immediately. This would permit a more extended service test to be made and a greater tooling on the part of the manufacturer of the bottleneck axle item. While the procurement of only 500 vehicles would not permit adequate axle tooling by the Spicer Company, the purchase of 1,500 vehicles would allow for such tooling to the extent of providing for thirty to fifty vehicles a day. A decided advantage thus would be gained should mass production at a later date become necessary.

The subcommittee held that to allot the entire proposed order for 1,500 jeeps to one manufacturer would "limit the Army to the development of a single type of vehicle which may not be the most satisfactory of the three types offered." If, however, the procurement were split among Bantam, Ford, and Willys on the basis of 500 each, the field of development would be extended, production would not be delayed, and additional potential sources for mass production would be made available.

Informal quotations already secured from the three manufacturers for 500 jeeps apiece revealed that Bantam's price was $1,123 per unit; Ford's $1,130; and Willys' $1,581.38. On the basis of these bids, the subcommittee thought that $1,250 was a fair estimate of what the maximum cost of each truck should be, and recommended that the Quartermaster General be authorised to negotiate contracts for 500 each with Bantam, Ford and Willys on the above terms. It also suggested that the Spicer Company be notified of this procurement and be guaranteed an outlet for 1,500 sets of axles and transfer cases[8].

Representatives of the using arms at the meeting, however, did not look with a favourable eye on the plan to bring Ford and Willys into the programme. Positive non-concurrence to the subcommittee's report were entered by the Infantry and Field Artillery. The Cavalry concurred only on the basis of the inclusion of certain specified conditions advocated by that service.

In his official non-concurrence, the Infantry member gave several reasons for his inability to agree with the majority's conclusions and recommendations. In his opinion the proposed programme would not provide the number of jeeps required by the Infantry for replacement of the motorcycle with sidecar, procurement of which was then in suspense pending the adoption of a substitute. The procedure adopted, he thought, would "inevitably result in delay beyond that justified at this time." Since the axles and transfer cases used in the jeep were the only feature essentially distinguishing it from other vehicles in this general class, and since there was only one source available for these components, he could not see how the

35

apportionment of the order among the three manufacturers would extend the field of development to any considerable extent. On the contrary, it might result in restricting the field, "since it is understood that failure to support the manufacturer who has developed this vehicle with adequate contracts may result in the elimination of that source entirely."

The Infantry representative objected to the purchase from Ford and Willys of a thousand vehicles "which have never been seen, much less tested," especially since there already had been developed a vehicle—the Bantam—that "has been engineered, thoroughly tested, and found satisfactory." In this regard he cited previous positions of the Quartermaster General on procurement by negotiation to the effect "that there could be no negotiation of a contract if the manufacturer concerned had not previously produced a satisfactory vehicle." If that principle was valid in respect to the half-ton truck and the motorcycle, the Infantry held that it should be considered valid in the case of the jeep.

In defending the cause of the original producer, the Infantry member stated that Bantam was the only manufacturer that had built the jeep according to the wishes of the Army. "It is the only instance," he declared, "known to the undersigned of any vehicle manufacturer co-operating to this extent. The past attitude of both the other concerns . . . has been one of indifference to the special requirements of the military service, until the subject vehicle had been designed and had demonstrated its potentialities . . . It does not seem either in the interest of the government or consistent with fair play to discourage them [Bantam] and others in such efforts by failing to give them the support to which their initiative and co-operative attitude entitle them."

For the foregoing reasons, the Infantry recommended that the 1,500 trucks for the extended development and service test be purchased by negotiation from Bantam at a unit cost of not more than $1,000. The way was to be left open, however, for the submission of pilot models by any other manufacturers wishing to enter this field. These models were to be given tests equal to those already conducted with the Bantam jeep, and upon satisfactory completion of such tests and approval of the vehicle by the using arms, the manufacturers concerned were to be included in any future negotiations for procurement[9].

The non-concurrence of the Field Artillery agreed with the Infantry that the American Bantam Company should be given the entire order and that no contracts should be entered into with Willys and Ford until they had produced satisfactory pilot models. The Chief of Field Artillery wished it known that "he has consistently objected and still objects, to contracting for the purchase of motor vehicles until a suitable pilot has been produced, tested, and accepted by the government[10]. The concurrence of the Cavalry in the report of the subcommittee was based principally on the conditions that contracts with Ford and Willys be negotiated only *after* the pilot models' tests and approval by the using arms; that 500 jeeps be ordered from Bantam at once, and that production and delivery must not be delayed[11].

In submitting the report of the Motor Transport subcommittee to the General Staff, the Quartermaster General's concurrence in its recommendations was made subject to the prior approval, and acceptance of pilot models, no delay in the production of the 1,500 vehicles, and the submission by each manufacturer of "prices and deliveries on additional quantities on the basis of 2,500, 5,000, 7,500 and 10,000 vehicles, these prices and deliveries to be binding should it be found desirable to extend contract[12]."

Attached to the memorandum of the OQMG was a letter from Willys' sales director to the Holabird purchasing and contract officer, dated 18 October, and stating: "After talking to you Wednesday concerning our price, as compared to Bantam and since hearing that Ford had put in prices that are based on additional lots of the $\frac{1}{4}$-ton 4x4's . . . I asked our factory to get out their sharpest pencil and gamble on a volume basis . . ." Willys then reduced their previous price offer from $1,581.39 to $1,235.00[13].

The decision of the Secretary of War and the General Staff in this initial skirmish between the using arms and the Quartermaster Corps was that the entire 1,500 trucks were to be procured from American Bantam; that future procurement was to be based upon prior submission and acceptance of pilot models; and that the Spicer Company was to be notified of the purchase and guaranteed the outlet for the 1,500 axles and transfer cases that would be needed. Classification of the truck was to be "Required type, Development type, Service Test article".[14]

Exception to the above directive was taken immediately by the Quartermaster General's Office. In a second endorsement dated 1 November and signed by the Quartermaster General, reconsideration of the General Staff's action was requested. It was stated that the information about the decision of the General Staff had been conveyed to the Washington sales representative of the Bantam Company in advance, enabling him to inform both Holabird and his competitors even before the OQMG received the official notification from the Adjutant General. This, the Quartermaster General felt, had already affected vendor relations.

Furthermore, the directive was seen as upsetting completely the "carefully considered plan" of the QMC to split the order for the 1,500 jeeps "between two or three companies" in order to ensure proper engineering development and to provide for adequate productive facilities. The probable requirements for the jeep were seen as not less than 11,800 before 30 June, 1941, and it was "the considered opinion of the Quartermaster General's office that the American Bantam Car Company cannot furnish these requirements and ensure a continuing service organisation." In support of this contention the OQMG noted the precarious financial condition of this company, pointing out that Bantam had wanted an advance payment of thirty per cent or $52,000 on the original contract for the seventy-odd jeeps. It also quoted the statement in the Infantry's non-concurrence to the effect that failure on the part of the Government to support Bantam might result in its entire elimination. It struck again at the firm's finances with the statement: "The unusual amount of publicity released by the American Bantam Company considered in conjunction with the present financial situation of the company give cause for suspicion that the possibility of Army contracts is being used as a basis for stock promotion."

Replying to the objections of the using arms which, it was implied, had probably had some effect on the General Staff's decision, the endorsement insisted that any rejection of the subcommittee's recommendations based upon the fact that Ford and Willys had not yet submitted pilot models, was not justified since the Quartermaster General had specifically precluded any such negotiations except on that basis. Nor did the OQMG agree with the using arms that the production might be delayed. On the contrary, "this proposed programme was specifically designed to expedite the procurement of the eventual requirements," since either Ford or Willys was expected eventually to produce axles and transfer cases, thus breaking the Spicer bottleneck. Moreover, commitments had already been made by the Quartermaster Corps with Ford and Willys for engineering and development, and expenditures by the two firms for this work had been encouraged.

Finally, the Quartermaster General's Office felt that the award of the entire contract to Bantam was "contrary to the spirit and letter of the general principles governing the letting of defence contracts, particularly with respect to the effect of any Army programme upon the peacetime economy."

The above arguments failed to sway the General Staff from its directive. None of them was deemed to outweigh the considerations responsible for its original decision. The General Staff did not consider it "advisable to delay procurement of the Bantam, which has been found suitable, pending service tests of other makes; neither is it considered feasible to order a large quantity of cars from a manufacturer prior to completion of test of a pilot model." Since recommendations for the purchase of vehicles from Ford and Willys would be entertained upon satisfactory completion of tests of their pilot models, development of additional production facilities would not be prevented. "In view of the foregoing," the third endorsement concluded, "the directive contained in the 1st Endorsement is reaffirmed and will be executed." [15]

At this point it appeared as though the using arms were going to emerge victorious over the Quartermaster Corps. But the QMC was not through contending for its viewpoint and policy. On the day following receipt of the General Staff's refusal to reconsider its original decision, another memorandum, over the Quartermaster General's signature, was transmitted direct to General R.C. Moore, Deputy Chief of Staff, G-4[16]. It acknowledged receipt of the directive and stated that the QMC would now see about obtaining the 1,500 jeeps from the Bantam Company, at the same time stating: "Of course, you understand that this proposal must be approved by the National Defence Advisory Commission[17] before an award can be made." The Quartermaster General wished to go on record that he did not consider the directed action in the best interests of the Government. Again pointing out that Bantam was a small company with no important productive facilities, the OQMG considered that "their financial status is entirely inadequate for any substantial production programme." By contrast, the facilities and financial standing of both Ford and Willys were such that "there is no question of their ability to produce cars in volume if the War Department so desires." The Quartermaster General regretted very much that the War Department should embark on a procurement programme "with a company which has no national organisation and is not prepared to render any service on the vehicles purchased."

Understanding that the decision of the Assistant Chief of Staff was based on the belief that Bantam could produce the 1,500 jeeps more quickly than if the order were split between the three manufacturers, the Quartermaster General could not "but feel that this decision is based on misinformation furnished by the representative of the Bantam Company." The OQMG had made every effort to expedite the development and procurement of these vehicles and had its plan been adopted without delay when first presented, jeeps would have started to flow in January. Spicer would have been in production on axles and transfer cases to each of the three companies at the rate of ten to sixteen a day, and the Ford and Willys pilot models would have been received, tested, and put into production as fast as Spicer could furnish the axles and transfer cases. Unfortunately, the Quartermaster plan had not been adopted, thus causing the delay, and the best production guarantee that now could be had from Spicer was fifty sets per day starting on the tenth of the following March. By that time the pilot model tests of Ford and Willys would "have easily been completed and those companies will be ready to produce vehicles at a much more rapid rate than the Bantam Company can hope to do..." The Quartermaster General doubted "the ability of the Bantam Company to turn out 50 cars a day, even if axles are provided, without additional financing and expansion of their present facilities," whereas there could be no question of the production ability of Ford and Willys[18].

The memorandum contended that the Quartermaster General's Office was just as much interested as the using arms in the procurement and rapid delivery of satisfactory vehicles, "and due to the fact that we are continually in touch with changing conditions in the automobile industry and in a position to affect these conditions by virtue of orders placed, it would seem that this office is better qualified to exercise judgement on matters such as these, than are those who are dependent upon information and sometimes misinformation from limited sources."[19] Therefore, the Quartermaster General wished to reiterate his recommendation "that the award to the Bantam Company be confined to 500 vehicles and that authorisation be given ... to place the additional 1,000 with the Ford Motor Company and/or Willys-Overland, Inc., upon the completion of satisfactory pilot model tests and in such a manner so as not to delay the procurement of the entire 1,500."

A few days after the despatch of this memorandum to the Deputy Chief of Staff, the Bantam Company wrote a letter to Brigadier General Joseph E. Barzynski, Chief of the QMC Motor Transport Division[20], in which it said that the company's attention had been called to "the fact that certain false rumours, without foundation, have been circulated regarding the labour conditions, production facilities, equipment, etc., of the American Bantam Car Company, Butler, Pennsylvania." In refutation of these rumours, the letter cited "some facts which will discredit these mis-statements." It was claimed there was no lack of skilled labour to man the plant; the company was prepared to make future delivery on time, "as in the past", and noted that it was equipped to furnish bonds in this connection; its experience in building midget cars was greater than that of any other manufacturer in the country; and its facilities and production capacity were such that the order for 1,500 jeeps would not even require the total output of its plant. For confirmation of these statements, General Barzynski was referred to Mr. A.J. Brandt of both the Ordnance Department and the National Defence Commission. Mr. Brandt was said to have purchased all of Bantam's machinery, to have laid out its production line, and to know more about the company from an engineering standpoint than anyone else. A complete set of blueprints and photographs of the Bantam factory showing facilities, placement of machinery and equipment, etc., was attached to the letter, which concluded with the request to be allowed to combat any other "false rumours that might come to the Quartermaster Corps regarding the Bantam Company."

Nevertheless, the Quartermaster Corps continued to press for the accomplishment of its aims in connection with the jeep. As it had implied it might do in its memorandum to General Moore, the QMC took its case straight to the National Defence Advisory Commission where it was reviewed by Commissioner Knudsen and John D. Biggers. They agreed with the QMC recommendation for the splitting of the jeep order, but not entirely for all of the reasons advanced by the OQMG. In the words of Mr. Biggers before the Truman Committee one year later, they did not believe that Bantam necessarily "was too weak and small to handle that order," but that "it was advisable for the military services to have at least two sources of supply qualified to make every important vehicle in the event of an emergency, because the demands might overnight expand far beyond the demand of the present ..."[22].

While recognising that either Bantam, Ford or Willys could take care of the Army's jeep requirements as of that time, Mr. Biggers pointed out that the Defence Commission had definitely favoured the policy of multiple sources of supply for other motor vehicles as well as for the $\frac{1}{4}$-ton right from the start. This he found "interesting" because in the cases of the 1½ and 2½-ton trucks, the Quartermaster Corps, in the interest of standardisation and simplification of the field maintenance problems, had recommended that all future orders be given on a negotiated contract basis to the current suppliers of these vehicles, which were the Chevrolet and Yellow Coach divisions of General Motors. These had become the sole suppliers, respectively, of the 1½ and 2½-ton trucks strictly through competitive bidding. Despite his previous association with General Motors, Commissioner Knudsen felt that the policy desired by the QMC was not wise and that a second source for each of these vehicles ought to be provided. To that extent, therefore, he had even gone against the interests of the company with which he had been closely connected[23].

From this it can be seen that motor transport policy on this point was in an unsettled state at the time, with the Quartermaster Corps favouring single sources for the 1½ and 2½-ton trucks, yet advocating more than one source for the jeep[24]. It must be remembered, however, that the ¼-ton had not yet been standardised and that the QMC was on record as desiring further development in the field by Ford and Willys, despite the using arms' willingness to settle on the Bantam model that had been tested by them and found satisfactory. The importance of keeping in mind this difference in policies for different trucks and manufacturers will become apparent later on in this story of the procurement of the jeep, for when the first really big order for 16,000 of these trucks came up for consideration the following year, the Quartermaster Corps, for standardisation reasons, reversed its previous policy of more than one source for the jeep and urged that the entire order be given to Ford on a negotiated contract.

The intervention of the Defence Commission in the controversy over the procurement of the 1,500 jeeps now caused the Deputy Chief of Staff to compromise his last decision. At a conference in General Moore's office, Mr. Biggers personally explained the Commission's viewpoint. As he further put it in his testimony before the Truman Committee, "We went into it and agreed with the Quartermaster Corps that division between at least two sources was desirable. We didn't recommend which two. We took our views to the Deputy Chief of Staff and explained them. We didn't argue for any company. We argued merely for Bantam and one other, not for two others."[25] Thereupon General Moore decided that 4,500 jeeps would be purchased instead of the 1,500 contemplated originally, and that Bantam, Ford, and Willys would be given orders for 1,500 each subject to approval of their pilot models.

This compromise settlement was communicated by letter from Biggers to the Quartermaster General on 14 November[26]. In it was included the authorisation for negotiation of a contract with Bantam for 1,500 jeeps at a unit cost of $955.59 less one per cent for payment in ten days[27]. The letter also suggested that since Ford had offered to loan certain tool equipment to Spicer to expedite the delivery of axles and transfer cases, full advantage should be taken of this offer, "and if the Ford and Willys pilot models merit prompt approval we believe that maximum early deliveries to the armed services could be best accomplished by some equitable division of the axle production between the three manufacturers."

Negotiations were now undertaken with Ford and Willys. Ford offered to furnish 1,500 jeeps at a price of $975 less $50 per vehicle for payment within thirty days. If its pilot model was accepted within three weeks of presentation for test, delivery of the first 400 vehicles would be made on or before 10 March, 1941, and the remaining 1,100 by 15 April[28]. Verbal approval of this offer was obtained from the Assistant Chief of Staff, G-4, on 18 November, and ASW approval of the proposed contract for $1,387,500 was requested the following day[29]. Clearance through both the ASW and the Defence Commission was immediate and the Ford Motor Company was also notified of the award by Holabird on the same day, 19 November. On 28 November, however, the Quartermaster General was ordered by the Assistant Secretary of War to halt immediately the preparation of the formal written instrument embodying the above agreement. The entire matter then hung fire for more than two weeks, and on 19 December, Lt. Colonel Dow of the OQMG was requested by the OASW "to prepare immediately for General Gregory's signature a memorandum of the 'compelling reasons' why an award should be made to the Ford Motor Company." In the event that the Quartermaster General's signature would cause any delay, the signature of Colonel Dow was to suffice. Accordingly, Colonel Dow prepared the requested memorandum which was transmitted to the Assistant Secretary of War on 20 December. The reasons for making this award, Colonel Dow said, were the same as set forth by the Quartermaster General in his previous correspondence with the General Staff on the subject. The Quartermaster General's second endorsement of 2 October 1940, and his memorandum of 6 November to General Moore were quoted at length. It was pointed out further, that Ford's offer was the best received so far and that as a result of the steps already taken "the Ford Company now has a legal and binding contract in the form of an offer and an acceptance."[30] Finally, on 27 December, Holabird was notified by the OQMG that the Ford contract had been reviewed and again approved by the Assistant Secretary of War and was now released for execution.[31]

Newspaper Attacks on Alleged WD-Ford "Deal"

It is possible that among the reasons for the hesitation and delay in clearing the final execution of the Ford contract, was the uproar that arose from certain elements of the Nation's press, especially the so-called pro-labour and liberal organs such as Marshall Fields PM, and The Nation. The former publication was especially denunciatory of the proposed award to Ford. In its 14 December issue there appeared a despatch from Washington over the signature of I.F. Stone, in which it was flatly charged that on the pending Ford contract for approximately $1,400,000 worth of jeeps, "certain officials of the Defence Commission and the War Department have gone out of their way to favour Ford." Ford, it was claimed, "is being permitted to 'muscle in' and reap the benefit of an important new development in mechanised warfare, with great peacetime potentialities, although the Army itself and a small manufacturer co-operating with the Army did the pioneering."

Referring to the history of the small-car idea for the Army, Stone said that the midget car "was scoffed at in military circles until the German attack on the Low Countries and France showed that the Nazis were using a similar vehicle. The Quartermaster Corps remained sceptical until Charles H. Payne, assistant to the head of the Bantam Automobile Company at Butler, Pennsylvania, managed to reach Harry Woodring, then Secretary of War. Woodring saw the possibilities in this midget military vehicle." Now that the vehicle was a proven success, and because Ford had yet to meet the Army's specifications for the jeep, Ford and his friends on the Defence Commission and in the War Department were exerting pressure to have the weight specifications changed "to meet what Ford can produce rather than what the Army needs." The Ford jeep then being developed was said to be about 200 pounds heavier than the tentative weight specifications set around this time at 2,000 pounds. The Willys jeep was claimed to be about 400 pounds too heavy. Yet a contract for Ford had already been cleared and the next move, Stone predicted, was to be an attempt by Ford to get another upward revision of the weight specification.

The article further attacked the award to Ford from the labour angle. It noted that the labour policy of the Defence Commission issued 31 August, specifically mentioned the Wagner Act as one of the statutes to be adhered to on defence contracts. "Ford," wrote Stone, "with no fewer than six Labour Board decisions outstanding against him, one of them already upheld in the United States Circuit Court, is the country's foremost violator of the Wagner Act. Yet he has just been awarded his second contract." On the other hand, it was pointed out that Bantam was a small concern in need of the defence order, and that Butler, Pennsylvania, needed the extra employment. To get the order to that concern "would spread defence work, reward a small manufacturer for co-operating with the Army, make it unnecessary to award another defence contract to a Wagner Act violator." Representatives of labour on the Defence Commission were said to be incensed over the award to Ford, and a bitter behind-the-scenes fight was reported to have taken place. Even many ranking Army officers, according to Stone, were "disgusted" with what was going on.

"Behind Ford's eagerness to get the contract," declared the writer, "is the hope that after the war this midget car can be developed into an all-purpose farm machine which can pull a plough by day and take the family to the movies at night. The 'bottleneck' is the Spicer axle used in these cars, and the next step will be an attempt to obtain priority for Ford on the axles. This contract though cleared by the Defence Commission, cannot take effect until Ford meets Army specifications or the specifications are changed. There is still time to show labour that the Defence Commission and the War Department intend to keep their promises."[32]

The pro-labour newspaper fight against the Ford contrct continued for the next two months. In a follow-up article appearing in both *The Nation* and *PM* at the end of the year, Stone reiterated his previous charges.[33] He named John D. Biggers, president of the Libby-Owens-Ford Glass Company,[34] as Ford's "outstanding friend" on the Defence Commission, where Biggers had been serving as an executive assistant to Production Chief Knudsen. Although Ford was said to be "bringing to bear all the influence he can muster . . . in the Quartermaster Corps to get the specifications changed," no specific QMC personnel were mentioned by Stone as being directly connected with Ford. But the General Staff, wrote Stone, "never wanted to give this contract to Ford anyway, but were forced to do so by pressure from Ford's friends on the Defence Commission." The award of a similar contract to Willys was merely intended to "make it look less like favouritism to Ford."

The article declared that since the price of 1,500 jeeps to be made by Ford included the cost of tooling required to produce them, Ford would "thus have cost-free tooling for civilian production after the emergency is over." As a result of all this pressure on behalf of Ford, an unnecessary burden was being placed on the country's machine tool facilities "at a time when unfilled orders for essential arms machinery have created what is our most serious defence bottleneck." Since Bantam, with most of its workers idle or on part-time work, was equipped to handle all of the Army's needs as of that time, the special tooling that Ford and Willys would have to undergo was unnecessary duplication, it was claimed.

A United Press story carried in *The Nation* of 30 December, quoted R.J. Thomas, president of the CIO United Automobile Workers of America, as having said that the Ford contract would do grave damage to the morale of labour working on defence contracts. According to the despatch this award for $1,387,500 worth of jeeps was being given to Ford over the protest of Sidney Hillman, labour member of the Defence Commission. "Labour," the interview reported Thomas to have said, "has been asked to shoulder its full responsibility toward national defence . . . We have met those requests. At the same time, the most notorious and consistent violator of the Wagner Act is favoured with a defence contract by the Government whose laws are being violated . . ."[35]

Answering a request of 5 January 1941, from Mr. Biggers, Colonel Van Deusen of the QMC Motor Transport Division offered refutation to certain of the charges made in Stone's article of 30 December. "The question of Ford's compliance with the specifications," said Van Deusen, "has never been injected into the matter of the consummation of the contract. The provisions of the negotiations were that the production vehicles, insofar as design and delivery are concerned, would comply with changes directed by the War Department in the pilot model as submitted. This is no bar to the signing of the contract." It was denied that Ford had brought influence to bear in the QMC to have the specifications changed. Ford acknowledged that its pilot model was overweight, but the actual weight limitation for the production jeep was to be based on the result of the pilot model test. "The weight applicable to both the Ford and Willys model was tentatively set at 2,160 lbs, with the concurrence of the using services in a 'trade' in the negotiations of the added weight allowance versus a lower silhouette," reported Van Deusen. Additional weight was seen as representing "increased sturdiness and modifications determined as necessary from testing." This was just as true of the Bantam which now weighed 2,030 pounds as it was of the Ford model.

In respect to Stone's assertion that the General Staff had not wanted Ford to have the contract but had succumbed to outside pressure, Colonel Van Deusen stated that Motor Transport's original proposal to bring Ford and Willys into the jeep programme, at that time had been "verbally approved" by General Staff representatives. When the decision was made to set aside the QMC recommendation, the Quartermaster General entered a protest against it.

The charge that a totally unnecessary burden would be placed on the country's machine tool facilities at this critical time, was "entirely incorrect," the memorandum declared. On the contrary, the bringing of Ford into the picture would materially assist the machine tool situation, since Ford had actually loaned machine tools to Spicer to expedite the production of axles and transfer cases. In the case of Bantam, however, priorities had to be resorted to in order to provide it with tools.

To the argument that Bantam was equipped to handle all the Army's present needs and that the duplication of tooling by Ford and Willys was unnecessary, it was replied that "Bantam's potential production is much less than that of either Ford or Willys-Overland and an increase entails additional tooling costs in either case. Despite Bantam's inclusion in the price of the original 70 units of a considerable portion of tooling costs Ford's prices were lower than Bantam's. Bantam was paid and paid well for tooling for the manufacture of the original pilot model. Both Ford and Willys-Overland produced the pilot model without additional expense to the Government."

The memorandum concluded with the argument that of the several factors involved in the desire of the Quartermaster Corps to have Ford enter the ¼-ton field, three stood out: the "doubtful" financial status of Bantam as evidenced by both advance payments on the contract for the 70 jeeps and loans by the RFC; the previous lack of any use in the current procurement programme for motor vehicles of Ford's vast potential productive capacity in the lighter truck category; and "a desire to utilise Ford production capacity without complicating the standardisation achieved through award of contracts for the other types that Ford normally produces, i.e. ½-ton and 1½-ton classes."[36]

Continuing to hammer at the alleged "deal" between Ford and the War Department, another article by I.F. Stone appeared in the Sunday issue of PM on 19 January. It was asserted by Stone that his previous predictions to the effect that the weight specifications of the jeep would be changed to please Ford had been proven correct, since the Quartermaster Corps, over the objections of military experts, had now definitely raised the weight to 2,160 pounds, "or the lowest weight Ford's engineers have yet proposed to achieve." Bantam, whose jeep weighed 2,030 pounds when loaded with ten gallons of petrol and oil, had now been instructed to raise the weight of certain parts of its car to this figure on the order for 1,500. According to War Department officials with whom Stone claimed to have spoken "off the record", the usefulness of any midget car weighing more than 2,000 pounds would be impaired.

Stone further declared that Ford had succeeded in getting priority on axles, with Spicer to start delivery to that concern on 1 February. Bantam now would have to wait five to six weeks for its axles and hence would be unable to fulfil the terms of its contract. "Mr. Ford," wrote the author, "has won another victory behind the scenes in his fight to take this midget car away from the manufacturer who developed it."[37]

The controversy had now reached the point where a Congressional investigation by the House Military Affairs Committee was threatened.[38] It was reported in PM that the resolution would be introduced in a few days by Representative Faddis of Pennsylvania, a member of the committee. The story quoted Representative Faddis as follows: "There is nothing in Henry Ford's record to indicate that he's interested in national defence. His interest is in getting this work away from Bantam and developing a new light car after the war. He wants to make sure that Bantam won't be in the field to compete with him when he does. I see no reason to split this work up among several manufacturers, especially since Bantam is idle and there is unemployment in Butler, Pa., where its plant is situated. It has shown that it can build the midget car in a way that is satisfactory to the Army, and standardisation would be ensured by leaving the job in Bantam's hands.

The great problem in the field is to have a standard car. The problem of repairs and replacements becomes a nightmare when there are too many different types of cars in service."[39]

The Willys Jeep

Not only the Ford version of the jeep, but the Willys model as well was involved in the question of overweight. The problem was even more serious in the Willys case because its model weighed even more than the Ford jeep, and this undoubtedly had much to do with the Quartermaster Technical Committee's approval of still further increases in the weight specification.

As in the case of Ford, negotiations with Willys had begun immediately following the compromise decision of General Moore to buy 1,500 jeeps from each of the three manufacturers. Indicative of the close competition between the three makers in regard to price, was Willys' per unit quotation of $959 less one per cent for cash within ten days. This figure, Willys said, was based on a "gamble" as they claimed that their actual cost, without profit or overhead, was $989 per truck.[40] Willys' price was thus a scant three dollars more per unit than Bantam's and around twenty-four dollars more than the Ford quotation of $975 less $50 for payment in thirty days. The final net prices of all three were: Ford $925; Bantam $946.04; and Willys $949.41.[41]

The Willys price, like the others, included tooling costs, and 100 days after receipt of the order was required by them to get into production. Their rate of delivery was set at ten a day for the first week; twenty a day for the second week; and fifty a day until completion of the order. "If orders were released today [27 November] we could start 6 March," the Willys letter said.

Verbal approval of this award to Willys was obtained by Colonel Dow from Colonel Aurand, G-4, 3 December,[43] and clearance was immediately requested from the Assistant Secretary of War's Office. In a supplementary communication to the ASW dated 5 December, it was noted that although Willys' price was $3.39 higher per jeep than Bantam's, consideration should be given to the fact that the two vehicles, while similar, were not identical, being development types. Furthermore, Bantam had had the opportunity of writing off a large portion of their tooling cost on their original order for sixty-two jeeps at a price of $2,415.50 each. While it also was true that Willys' price was $24.41 more per unit than Ford's, the Quartermaster General's Office believed "the statement . . . that their actual cost without profit or overhead is $989.00, to be correct." The Willys offer therefore was considered reasonable, and approval was requested, contingent, of course, upon the test and acceptance of its pilot model.[44]

But the Willys jeep could not be released for manufacture because the pilot model had failed to meet the weight conditions; hence there was no chance of production getting started by the following March.

The pilot model had arrived at Holabird on 13 November. The official inspection report disclosed the total weight of the Willys jeep to be 2,520 pounds—1,230 pounds in the front and 1,290 pounds in the rear. The gross weight was still higher, totalling 3,120 pounds, divided between the front and rear on the basis of 1,285 and 1,835 pounds, respectively. The gross weights were taken with a payload of 600 pounds including the driver.[45]

Like any other pilot model submitted for test, the Willys jeep took quite a battering from the Holabird course. As an example of the extreme punishment to which pilot models were subjected, the frame of the Willys fractured after 5,184 miles of operation; cylinders were badly worn after 5,011 miles, and the entire engine was replaced by a used motor taken from a Willys American, which also failed after 1,316 additional miles; the cooling system showed an excessive rise in temperature; at 6,109 miles, the transfer case main shaft bearings failed; the steering pin mounted on the front axle went out after 1,814 miles; spring failure was encountered throughout the test, and several other faults were noted.[46] The report was forwarded to the Quartermaster General by Colonel J. Van Ness Ingram of Holabird on 9 January, with the request for the swiftest possible action from the Adjutant General's Office so that Willys could be authorised to proceed with the contract. Willys itself was notified through a copy of the report of the deficiencies in its model that would have to be corrected.[47]

On 22 January 1941, three days after the appearance of the *PM* article containing what was apparently advance information on the increase of the jeep's weight to 2,160 pounds, the Quartermaster Corps Technical Committee met and considered the motor subcommittee's action and report on the Willys pilot model. The consensus of opinion among the members of the subcommittee present was that the maximum weight, without the machine-gun base and with 5.50-16 inch tyres, should not exceed 2,160 pounds; it was agreed to change the military characteristics accordingly. The Technical Committee accepted the subcommittee's opinion on the weight question and moved, seconded, and carried the motion to report to the Adjutant General:

a. That no sastisfactory pilot model has been submitted by the Willys-Overland Company to date, and that therefore the present requirements and authorisation be used for the purchase of the total 4,500 vehicles from the two concerns which have submitted satisfactory pilot models, these being the Ford Motor Company and the American Bantam Company, and that the contract of the Willys-Overland Company become operative upon acceptance by the Quartermaster Technical Committee of the pilot model from this company, which must be within the weight restriction of 2,160 pounds without machine-gun base and with 5.50-16 inch tyres.

b. It is further recommended that consideration be given to procuring this type vehicle at once for all the requirements of the Army.

Note: In this connection, it was pointed out that this is an attempt to prevent lag in production between this 4,500 vehicles and the next order.

c. The Committee further recommends that this type vehicle be classed as: Required Type, Adopted Type, Standard Type.[48]

Subsequently, minutes of the Quartermaster Corps Technical Committee, dated 27 June 1941, showed that on 11 June, the subcommittee had recommended to the full Committee adoption of the jeep's military characteristics, which were accepted on 16 June. But because of a meeting on the jeep requiring members of the Committee to journey to Forts Knox and Benning, the Committee had been informed by the Staff that the recommendations would not be acted on at that time. At the 27 June meeting the Technical Committee took up the matter of amending the military characteristics in compliance with the requirements of the Armoured Force and Infantry as developed at the Knox and Benning conferences. The previous action of the Committee taken in the 16 June meeting was now confirmed and the jeep recommended for classification as Required type, Adopted type, Standard.

On 7 February, General Moore, Deputy Chief of Staff, recommended to the Under Secretary of War that approval be given to the Willys contract. The reason for his decision, General Moore informed the Quartermaster General, was that he felt "an equity had been established in favour of the contractors, due to various conversations during the course of negotiations between the contracting officer and the contractor, and that this equity would be sustained in case of appeal to the Controller General." At the same time he emphasised that approval of military characteristics, or changes in them, was the prerogative of the Chief of Staff. In the case of the weight of the Willys model it appeared to Moore that the Quartermaster contracting officer had. in effect, "usurped the functions of the Technical Committee and the Chief of Staff in assuming military characteristics that have not been previously approved." The Quartermaster General was advised that when "it became apparent that it would be impracticable to obtain a satisfactory military vehicle with a minimum weight of 1,300 or 1,400 pounds, some other minimum weight should have been sought through proper channels as a change in military characteristics."[49]

In reply, the Quartermaster General denied that there had been or was any "intention . . . to usurp the functions of the Technical Committee or the Chief of Staff." The OQMG had considered the procurement of the 4,500 jeeps merely as an extension of the original purchase of seventy vehicles from Bantam. As such, the programme was but "a means of working out further revisions of military characteristics." The characteristics under which the initial seventy jeeps had been purchased were tentative only, and the adaptation of the commercial Bantam design, suggested on 19 June 1940, had been regarded as "merely a proposed goal for attainment, since no other similar vehicle had ever been built." It was pointed out to General Moore that the Technical Committee, while approving on 14 February 1941, an eighty per cent increase in the maximum weight originally recommended by the Ordnance subcommittee, had rejected "an additional 4.9% increase which would have permitted the Willys-Overland design to qualify for *future* contracts." This action of the Technical Committee said the Quartermaster General, had not been "accompanied by engineering data supporting its decision, and in the absence of thorough field service tests, there was nothing to indicate that the Willys design ultimately would not prove completely satisfactory."[50]

The notice to Willys instructing it to proceed with its contract was sent out by Holabird on 8 February and confirmed three days later by another letter stating:

With further reference to our letter of 8 February 1941, you are informed that, inasmuch as the pilot model vehicle submitted in connection with the subject contract has satisfactorily completed tests with the exception of the failure to meet the weight limitation of 2,160 pounds, and that the performance of the vehicle in spite of the added weight has been in all respects, equal to that required by the specifications, that your pilot model is accepted as suitable for military usage. It is, therefore, released for production with the other changes as indicated by the pilot model inspection report dated 8 January 1941.

Any modification or revision in the specifications covering future procurements will be based on the results obtained in the service tests of the three makes of vehicles now under procurement.[51]

The ever watchful and irrepressible Mr. Stone lost no time in bursting into print once more with the accusation that now that the weight specification had been lifted to 2,160 pounds to satisfy Ford, it was being increased again, this time to a *minimum* of 2,268 pounds, in order to meet the desires of Willys. He reported the using arms as declaring that 2,160 pounds was the absolute maximum weight they considered allowable. Bantam's representative, upon being informed of the proposed 2,268 pound minimum, was reported to have said, "I'll have to put pig iron in my car to make it heavy enough."[52]

During the balance of the jeep's career to July 1942 there were several other weight revisions. Both the military characteristics of June 1941 and the specifications of July 1941 showed the payload to have been raised to 800 pounds. The July specifications defined the payload as "800 pounds for operating personnel (including the driver) and military supplies." According to the specifications, "the weight of the truck, fully equipped (including lubricants and water), but *less* fuel, tyre chains and payload, shall not exceed twenty-one hundred (2,100) pounds for two (2) wheel steer trucks, and twenty-one hundred and seventy-five (2,175) pounds for four (4) wheel steer trucks, and every effort, consistent with best recognised

engineering practices, shall be made to minimise the weight."[53] By the end of August 1941, the motor subcommittee was recommending an increase of fifty pounds to take care of several additions and changes intended to improve the jeep, including a 40 ampere generator and other ignition equipment, an additional top support bow, a wheel puller, a drain cap on the petrol tank, lubrication provision for the universal joints, and box construction for the frame members from radiator to front bumper.[54] The final weight of the standardised jeep just before the QMC Motor Transport Service was transferred to Ordnance, was set as "Minimum consistent with service requirements. Weight fully equipped and serviced, with 6.00-16 tyres, less only payload, not to exceed 2,450 lbs."[55]

Other final characteristics as of that date were a towing capacity of 1,000 pounds; a minimum grade ability at gross weight of 60% without a towed load and 7% with a towed load; cross-country ability of operating, at gross weight and with towed load, over unimproved roads, trails, and open, rolling, and hilly country; a maximum speed of not less than 55 miles per hour on concrete and a minimum speed not greater than 3 m.p.h. at maximum engine torque; ability to ford water eighteen inches deep at minimum speed with fan operating; and a motor of at least four cylinders with a minimum displacement of 130 cubic inches. The dimensions included a maximum wheelbase of 80 inches and silhouette height of 40 inches; minimum axle ground clearance of 8 inches; and angles of approach and departure of not less than 45 and 35 degrees, respectively. Tyres were specified as 6.00-16, 6 ply, with heavy duty tubes, and the wheels were to be of the US Army standard divided type, including one spare wheel and tyre assembly. Military equipment included towing hooks on the two front corners or front bumper; a brush guard; and the US Army standard rear pintle, located so as to permit the towing of the 37 mm anti-tank gun. The electrical system consisted of "sealed beam" type headlights; standard combat zone safety lighting; ignition suppression equipment to prevent radio interference; a heavy duty voltage regulator; battery with negative ground; and a six-volt lighting, ignition, and starting system with the standard Army 40 ampere output generator. Other equipment included a collapsible windshield, suitable motor vehicle tools, chains, petrol and oil filters, shock absorbers on both axles, and brackets for mounting the standard shovel and axe. In respect to military service requirements, any design that rendered servicing, adjustment, and replacement difficult under field conditions was held to be not acceptable. The full floating axle was to be so constructed that if the axle shaft broke at any point the wheel would not come off. Steering drive ends were to be of the constant velocity joint type. Dull finish paint, reflecting as little light as practicable, was required throughout. Flexible brake line tubing was to be protected from damage by suitable guards. A reinforced frame was called for to provide for mounting the .50 calibre machine-gun on a pedestal mount. The fan was to be readily disconnected; there was to be complete interchangeability of parts; the jeep was to operate in a satisfactory manner on 60% longitudinal and 40% side slopes; and the body was to conform to the latest applicable drawing. Under the provisions of paragraph 13, AR 850-25, the classification of the jeep was shown to be: Required type, adopted type, Standard Article.[56]

Summarising the situation on the procurement of the 4,500 jeeps at the end of 1940, we find that Ford's price was lowest, Bantam was next, and Willys was high, although there was only $3.37 difference between its price and Bantam's. Since both the Ford and Willys models were overweight, the latter excessively so, the weight specifications had been changed accordingly.

Delivery schedules for all three as of this time showed Ford expected to produce 400 jeeps by 10 March 1941, and the remaining 1,100 by 15 April. Bantam was to turn over 950 units by 15 April and the balance of its 1,500 by 30 April. The Willys schedule called for 700 trucks by 15 April, 1,300 by 30 April and the entire 1,500 by 7 May.[57]

None of these schedules were fulfilled to the letter, however. As a result of its loan of machine-tool equipment to Spicer, Ford was enabled to start delivery on 8 February, at which time it shipped eight jeeps. Its volume shipment, however, did not start until 3 March. With the exception of two jeeps diverted to defence aid (lend-lease) requirements, Ford production was completed by 19 May 1941, one month behind the tentative schedule of December 1940. In addition to the controversy over the Ford contract, strikes at Spicer beginning 2 April and at Ford starting 4 April, both ending on 22 April, contributed to the delay.[58]

In the case of American Bantam, the final delivery date was extended to 2 July 1941, and the contract completed 26 June, six days ahead of the revised schedule but a month later than Ford. According to Mr. Fenn, 150 of the Bantam jeeps which were diverted for overseas shipment had to be accompanied by large quantities of spare parts that could only be obtained by tearing down eleven jeeps and boxing them as parts.[59] Bantam also had been affected by the Spicer strike and had so notified the QMC Motor Transport Division.[60]

While the time consumed in the settlement of the weight question hampered the production and deliveries of both Ford and Willys, it particularly affected the latter. The overweight of the Willys jeep was caused mainly by the heavier, more powerful "Go-Devil" engine which was standard in their regular commercial "Americar". This motor had a displacement of 139 cubic inches and was about 80 pounds heavier than either Bantam's or Ford's, which were 112 and 119 cubic inches respectively. Since the regular engine continued to be used, Willys was forced to reduce the weight of their model elsewhere. According to Colonel Van Deusen, this was accomplished by using a single die for the floor, slightly lighter gauges of sheet metal than used by Bantam or Ford in certain parts where no stress or strain was involved, and by careful clipping of unnecessary weight off bolts. All of this taking time, Willys was not able to start deliveries until 7 June[61], despite the orders of 8 and 11 February releasing its model for production, and was still at work on its initial order the following month, when the question of who was to get the first big order of 16,000 jeeps needed by the Army, arose to plague still further all of the personnel involved in the jeep controversy.

Comparative Tests of Bantam, Ford, and Willys Jeeps by Infantry Board

It will be remembered that the 1,500 jeeps from Ford and Willys over protests of the using arms, had been purchased and put into production without receiving the regular field service test, although the pilot models had been tested by the QMC at Holabird. The Infantry now decided to put the Ford and Willys production models through the same kind of service tests that had been given the original Bantam jeeps. Accordingly, on 12 May, the Adjutant General directed the Quartermaster General to divert one production jeep each from Ford and Willys to the Infantry Board. In the directive of the Chief of Infantry to the Board it was desired that "if practicable, one production model of the Bantam manufacture be included in these tests to such extent as may be necessary to compare its performance with the experimental models already tested, and to avoid erroneous conclusions which might be drawn from comparing the original and unmodified Bantam models with models of other makes in which many of the faults discovered in the original Bantam have been corrected." Only practical performance under all field conditions was to be considered. Refinement of design or appearance were to be disregarded except insofar as they affected practical utility.

The directive further noted that since the Ford and Willys jeeps were "copies of the original Bantam design", the three vehicles were essentially identical except for differences in the powerplant and certain other refinements of detail. Aside from the fact that the Ford light farm tractor motor had a slightly higher power-rating than the Continental used by Bantam, "a change in the shape of the hood resulting in recessed location for the headlights and a flat-topped hood, approved in advance by this office as satisfactory, is the only other substantial point of difference of this make from the Bantam." Pointing out that the heavier Willys motor, with a power rating of about thirty per cent more than the Bantam or Ford, required a still heavier transmission in order to take its greater torque, and that both the Ford and Willys motors were heavier than Bantam's, the Board was informed of the possibility that "in order to come within the maximum weight limitation of 2,160 lbs, lightening of other parts of the vehicles, especially in the frame, brush-guards, or in the thickness of the body may have been resorted to." If such lightening had a materially adverse effect upon vehicle ruggedness, it was to be reported. If it did not have such an effect "that fact should furnish the basis for recommending similar decrease in weight of other makes, and arriving at a standardisation of parts at minimum weights." Absolute differences in power output were considered to be unimportant "except as they affect practical performance across country or ... roadability at speeds below sixty-five miles per hour on smooth level roads."[62]

The Willys jeep arrived at Fort Benning, Georgia, on 26 June, and for comparison purposes, a Ford was obtained from the 8th Infantry and a Bantam from the 22nd Infantry. A partial report on the tests disclosd that the Willys jeep was superior in nearly all performance features, the Bantam second, and the Ford a poor third. On high gear acceleration the order of superiority was Willys, Bantam, Ford. The highest level road speed, 74 mph, was attained by the Willys, the Bantam reached a top of 64 mph, and the Ford's best speed was 59 mph. Three grades were selected to test grade climbing ability and here again the order of superiority was Willys, Bantam, and Ford. Bantam had the best score on fuel consumption, with an average of 23.2 miles per gallon over a speed range of 20 to 50 miles per hour, followed by Ford with 20.9 miles per gallon, and Willy last with 20.2 miles per gallon. Ford had the shortest turning radius with 17.2 feet, Willys was next with 19.4 feet, and Bantam last with 20.4 feet. Braking tests showed the Bantam superior insofar as quick stopping was concerned, and the Willys and Ford next in that order. In testing the cross country ability of the three jeeps, it was found that all could successfully negotiate swamp, eroded gulleys or various depths and widths including one about eight feet deep and fifteen feet wide, and slopes up to twenty-six degrees. In attempting to rush a slope of twenty-eight degrees in low ratio second gear, the Ford jeep failed to reach the top, and Bantam, while succeeding, had no reserve power left. The Willys jeep, however, topped the rise at a speed of 10 miles per hour, carrying a passenger in addition to the driver and sandload. The report stated it had a great reserve of available power.

In comparing the design features of the subject vehicles, the report found that the Willys had a superior engine of greater torque, a transmission with greater ease in shifting, a stronger frame, and a better radiator and top. Bantam had better steering, and both Ford and Bantam springs, mounted in rubber, were considered superior to Willys. Ford had the best handbrake, headlights, and seats. Willys and Ford were both disclosed to have better front brake line protection than Bantam and more satisfactory tyre carriers.

In summarising the results of the above tests, the report divided its findings into "favourable" and "unfavourable" comment on all three jeeps. The performance of the Willys, because of its great horsepower and torque, was held to be superior to the other two in acceleration, maximum speed, grade climbing, and cross country ability. In design, the Willys was superior in respect to engine, transmission, frame, and top. Bantam's two points of superiority were in its lower fuel consumption and shorter stopping distance. The Ford's arrangement of the gear shift lever, transfer case controls, and handbrake was the best, as was also its provision for greater leg room and driver comfort.

On the "unfavourable" side, the driver position of the Willys was found to be cramped and awkward due to short leg room and the location of the accelerator pedal. Its handbrake was in an awkward position and required a compound movement to apply and lock. The Willys gearshift lever, located on the steering column was thought to be more vulnerable to breakdown because of the additional linkage required. On severe slopes, failure of the Willys carburretor was noted. Unfavourable aspects of the Bantam were the inaccessability of the handbrake, difficulty in fastening the top, and failure of the carburettor on severe slopes. The performance of the Ford, in comparison with the Willys and Bantam, was considered "poor." In addition, shifting of the Ford gears was difficult, resulting in clashing; steering was unsatisfactory, a tendency for the car to wander being noted; the top was difficult to set up; and the carburettor also failed on severe slopes.

In general, the report stated that all of the subject vehicles were good and performed well across country and on roads, and that all were satisfactory, except for faulty carburettion and the unreliability of hydraulic brakes in cross country service. The report recommended, therefore, that besides the correction of the general faults disclosed by the tests, "the standard vehicle should be based upon the Willys chassis, with the Ford shift lever and handbrake arrangement, and performance characteristics of the Willys." It was also recommended that radio suppression equipment be provided.[63] Concurring in the conclusions and recommdations of its Test Section, the Infantry Board forwarded the report to the Chief of Infantry[64] whose office, in turn, transmitted it to the Quartermaster General, through the Adjutant General, for appropriate action.[65] When the report reached Holabird steps were taken to rectify the faults noted in the Willys jeep by the Infantry Board, and on 26 August the depot reported to the Quartermaster General that it believed "Willys-Overland has been required to eliminate all of the faults cited in the Infantry Board Report, with the exception of an alteration in driver's seat positioning, without regard to weight limitations." Holabird tests on seating positions, made with drivers ranging from 5'6" to 6'2" in height, had shown that every driver preferred the Willys seating arrangement. Furthermore, the Infantry representative, Lt. Col. Oseth, had appeared to favour the retention of the Willys seat when the matter was discussed with him on one of his visits to Holabird. The Holabird report made it clear that the additional features being demanded of Willys would require an additional weight allowance and therefore recommended that the specification weight limit "be increased by at least 50 pounds . . . to cover the added features not contemplated by the Willys-Overland bid and to allow for variations in component unit weight."[66] In forwarding the comments and recommendation of Holabird to the General Staff, the Office of the Quartermaster General called the Adjutant General's attention to its letter of 27 August in which approval was asked for the action of the QMC Technical Committee, taken at its meeting the day previous, recommending that the minimum weight allowance be increased by fifty pounds.[67]

Purchase of 16,000 Jeeps from Willys

In the meantime, early in July 1941, current directives to the Quartermaster General were calling for the immediate procurement of additional requirements for the now standardised jeep, amounting to 16,000 vehicles. Highlights of this procurement were to be the reversal of previous War Department policy and the stipulation of procurement conditions resulting eventually in the elimination of American Bantam from the jeep production programme; the championing of Ford by the Quartermaster Corps for the entire award despite the fact that Willys was the low bidder; the forcing of the contract to Willys by Director-General Knudsen of the Office of Production Management, which by now had replaced the old National Defence Commission; and the culmination of the entire wrangle in a congressional investigation by the Truman Committee—all of this taking place in one short month.

Picking up the procurement story of the jeep after the purchase of the 4,500, it became apparent in May 1941 that both Ford and Bantam would need additional contracts if production of jeeps was to be maintained at their plants, pending decision as to further procurements. While obviously not so important to Ford, which was loaded with other defence contracts, notably airplane, the need for more work at this time was serious in the case of the Bantam Company.

About 20 April, according to H.F. Fenn, president of Bantam, the Bantam plant was paid a visit by Major McAuliffe of G-4 and Mr. Curry of the Assistant Secretary of War's Office for the purpose of discussing with Fenn "the best way to keep the plant running," in order not to lose the "key men" who formed the nucleus of each assembling unit all the way along the assembly line. Stoppage of jeep production would break up and scatter these important groups of employees who alone had the necessary "know how" in respect of the production of the jeep. The visit of the two War Department representatives resulted in Bantam's production being cut down from the high of 65 units per day to about 15 units daily. "That," said Fenn, "was agreeable to us and was agreeable to the Army," since by this method the plant could be kept going and the services of the key men retained.[68]

On 23 May, the execution of negotiated contracts with both Bantam and Ford for 1,000 jeeps each, was authorised. The net unit price of the Bantam contract was $864.14 and the total contract consideration was $864,141.30. For Ford the net unit price was $865.70, but this included an additional $4.70 for 6.00-16 tyres. The total Ford contract amounted to $865,700.[69] On the basis of the Ford having 6.00-16 tyres, which were not shown for the Bantam award, Ford's unit price was actually lower than Bantam's. Although both of these contracts were negotiated, the increasing keenness of competition for jeep contracts again may be judged from the closeness of the above prices. Per unit cost of the jeep was to go still lower on the next procurement for 16,000, when the competitive bidding method was to be employed. Still later, however, after Bantam had been eliminated and the decision made to split all future contracts between Willys and Ford, negotiated contracts again were to be resorted to and the price of the jeep this time was to go up.

At the time this is being written—1943—it is easy to look back through the record of May 1941 and see that the position of American Bantam in the fight for contracts was already deteriorating rapidly. On the one hand there was Ford, apparent master of both the price and production situations, to be reckoned with. It seemed impossible that Bantam, heavily in debt to the RFC, could continue to compete with this Goliath. On the other hand, the comparative tests of all three jeeps that were to be completed within the next sixty days by the Infantry Board, would reveal the superior performance of the heavier, more powerful Willys model and thus give the Willys firm a strong advantage in that regard. Caught between Ford and Willys on both of these counts, the position of Bantam as a small producer was made even more untenable by the new policy of the War Department on the procurement of jeeps, announced early in July. For Bantam, the end was already in sight.

On 8 July, the Deputy Chief of Staff wrote the Under Secretary of War:

1. Reference the current directive to the Quartermaster General for the immediate procurement of initial requirements of the recently standardised truck, ¼-ton, 4x4, special attention is invited to two essentials for consideration in the procurement of this vehicle:

(a) It is essential that the design of these vehicles be frozen and that complete interchangeability of parts be secured in the further quantities procured during the period of the current emergency.

(b) The military situation is such that the delivery of these trucks into the hands of troops must be accomplished with the maximum possible speed.

2. In the placing of contracts for these vehicles by the Quartermaster Corps, it is essential that awards be made to manufacturers whose productive capacity is such as to assure delivery of the minimum requirements at the highest attainable rate of delivery. It is desired, if possible that these minimum requirements be secured for delivery within the succeeding six months.[70]

This new procurement policy was immediately communicated to the Quartermaster General by the Under Secretary in the following:

> Attached is a memorandum from General Moore to the effect that on the ¼-ton truck 4x4 it is essential that there be complete interchangeability of parts in the further quantities to be procured, and that deliveries be accomplished with the maximum speed within six months, if possible. Please be guided accordingly in the procurement of trucks of this type.[71]

The importance of these two directives on the procurement of the jeep at that time cannot be emphasised too much. For reasons which already have been explained at length, the stipulations set forth for the freezing of the design and complete interchangeability of parts meant that regardless of how these 16,000 jeeps were procured—whether by negotiated contract or by competitive bidding—it was almost a certainty that the design of only one manufacturer could be used, if the aim of the War Department for complete standardisation was to be achieved.[72]

This in turn meant that in all probability only the make whose design was selected would be in a position to produce the adopted vehicle within the short period of time specified in the General Staff's directive. For any other manufacturer to produce the same model, extensive retooling and machinery changes would be required. In short, from the policy of multiple sources for the further development of the jeep previously advocated by both the Quartermaster Corps and the National Defence Commission, the War Department, in the interests of standardisation, now reversed itself and cleared the way for the production of a jeep of one design from one source. A month later the Truman Committee was to manifest great curiosity over the allegedly hidden reasons behind this turnabout in policy.

Aside from the single design by one manufacturer plan, there was one other alternative method by which the standardisation conditions set by the General Staff could be met. This was to take the best features of the three jeeps and weld them into one standardised design that could be made by all three manufacturers, similar to the procedure used for the 'B' series trucks of 1918. As will be disclosed shortly, the Quartermaster Corps objected to this on the grounds that time was too short to permit the designing of such a standardised truck.

The choice of the Quartermaster Corps for the award of the contract for the 16,000 jeeps turned out to be the Ford Motor Company with which it wished to deal on a negotiated basis. This QMC proposal was refused approval by the OPM, whose attitude was best expressed in the following statement of John D. Biggers:

> . . . We in OPM—and that includes Mr. Knudsen and Mr. Hillman and Donald Nelson and myself—after going over this with the Under Secretary of War, reached an agreement in which he concurred that it was contrary to public policy to give that business to Ford if there were two other potential and, in our judgement, qualified producers, one of whom had in large measure originated the vehicle. We thought it was wrong to shut them out from bidding by a negotiated contract to a big producer who was already serving the Government and fulfilling contracts in many other fields. So the net result was that they [the QMC] said, 'What is the alternative?'
>
> We said, 'There are two alternatives. One, that you design a standard vehicle, such as the personnel carrier of the Ordnance Department, on which all three could bid.'
>
> The General Staff had insisted that these 16,000 vehicles be all identical, not from different models; so we said the only other alternative was that they should ask for bids and award the contract to the lowest bidder. They said they didn't have time to work out a standardised vehicle on which all three could bid, using this component, this engine, and that axle, and this transfer case and that transmission—that they didn't have time for that; so they asked for bids . . .[73]

Refusal of the OPM to approve the proposal of the Quartermaster Corps brought forth another memorandum from the OQMG to the Deputy Chief of Staff, General Moore. Reasons why the contract should be given to Ford again were cited. In order to procure these jeeps in the most satisfactory and expeditious manner, the Office of the Quartermaster General had particularly kept in mind the standardisation of parts, the ability of the manufacturer to supply maintenance parts in the future, and the contribution the manufacturer was able to make toward the breaking of such production bottlenecks as the constant velocity joints and transfer cases. "With these factors in mind," wrote the Quartermaster General, "it has been considered that the only company that now has the facilities and ability to contribute to production, coupled with actual experience in the manufacture of the critical item of constant velocity universal joints is the Ford Motor Company. Beyond all we have felt delivery was especially important. The only company which we believe can complete delivery quickly and satisfactorily is the Ford Motor Company."

The memorandum stated that when the matter was taken up with the Under Secretary of War, that official felt that he could not make the final decision regarding the procurement method to be used without prior consultation with the OPM. Representatives of the Quartermaster General met with Mr. Biggers in his office and notwithstanding "the arguments presented, direct negotiations with the Ford Motor Company have been disapproved by Mr. Biggers, on advice of Mr. Hillman and Mr. McKeachie. Subsequent instructions from the Under Secretary of War confirm this decision and direct that proposals be issued inviting informal competitive bidding."

"In accordance with our verbal understanding," continued the memorandum, "this office wishes to go on record to keep you advised of the developments in this matter and the fact that the procedure directed by the Office of Production Management and the Under Secretary of War will cause not only delay in time of delivery of this equipment, but is also expected to further complicate this highly controversial matter before it will be possible to place any contract.

"While it is recognised by all parties, due to the controversial nature of the matter, that there will be considerable debate, publicity and pressure applied in efforts to secure advantages for one or another of the potential manufacturers of this vehicle, it has been the hope of this office that it might be possible to get production under way before these factors could inject further delays into the procedure."[74]

In accordance with its instructions from higher authority, the Quartermaster Corps now proceeded to the business of obtaining informal competitive bids from interested manufacturers on an "all or none" basis. Four concerns submitted quotations: the three regular jeep makers and the Checker Cab Mfg. Corporation of Kalamazoo, Michigan. This company, although actually quoting the lowest per unit price, $736.53, of all four bidders, was given scant consideration because of the excessive delivery time required—almost nine months after date of award—and also because of Checker's qualification that even this delivery could not be fulfilled without preference certificates higher than could be offered by the Quartermaster Corps.[75]

The competition on the 16,000 award thus narrowed down to Bantam, Ford, and Willys, and it was here that Willys, unexpectedly enough in view of its previous high quotations, underbid Ford by almost thirty-four dollars per jeep. Willys was the lowest bidder with $748.74 per unit, Ford next with $782.59, and Bantam high with $788.32, six dollars more than Ford. Willys also offered the best delivery time with completion of the contract within 149 days after award, Bantam specified 152 days, and Ford was last with 171 days.[76]

Technical analyses by the Motor Transport Division of the three bids under consideration disclosed that Willys, like Checker, would require better priorities for its subcontractors than the A-1i rating then set for motor vehicles, particularly for Spicer, the supplier of axles, transfer cases, and universal joints. On the other hand, the next low bidder, Ford, had submitted letters from their major suppliers and statements of their own that indicated they would be able to meet their promised delivery on transfer cases and universal joints. Part of these would be obtained from Spicer "and their bid price included a charge for tooling in their own plant to increase the delivery possibilities of these parts." Bantam was said not to have supplied firm offers from all of its unit manufacturers and to have questioned its ability to delivery on an A-1i priority.

Based on the above analyses, it was felt that the bids of both Willys and Bantam did not give firm delivery promises and hence were "not for further consideration." The fact that Willys had not started delivery on its order for 1,500 jeeps until 7 June although they had been scheduled to start production on 14 March and would not complete this order until 4 August, whereas Ford had produced its quota by 19 May, was cited in substantiation of Motor Transport's contention that the award should go to Ford. Summing up, only Ford had made a firm offer as to delivery without qualification; it was the only maker that had included tooling costs in its bid for the alleviation of the axle and joint bottlenecks; the only facilties guaranteeing performance of the contract were possessed by Ford; and "by record of performance," only Ford could be expected to deliver service and spare parts concurrently with the vehicle. Noted also was the fact that Ford was "the only volume motor vehicle manufacturer which is not at present producing vehicles under the Quartermaster Corps motor programme." Therefore, despite Willys' low bid, it was recommended to the Quartermaster General that the award for the 16,000 jeeps be made to Ford at their net price of $782.59, totalling $12,521,440, and $1,657,107.26 additional for parts.[77] Requests for approval of the contract to Ford, including an option to increase the award by not more than fifty per cent within sixty days after the date of execution of the original contract, were submitted to the Under Secretary of War and the Director of Purchases, OPM, on 31 July.[78] While the award was approved by the War Department, the OPM again stepped in to block the transaction.

According to Biggers, he himself "refused to have anything to do with the award . . . because Willys-Overland, being a Toledo company, I wanted no part in the discussion . . . Mr. Knudsen decided the question, and when the War Department recommended the award of this contract to Ford at a $640,000 premium cost to the Government, Mr. Knudsen refused to approve it. He said that in his judgement as an automobile manufacturer, the low bidder [Willys] was a competent source of supply for that number of vehicles, and he wouldn't reject the low bid."[79]

As a result of the stand of the OPM on the matter, the Quartermaster General wrote the Under Secretary of War that the OQMG "has no other recourse but to recommend an award to the Willys-Overland Motors Incorporated for whom we have been advised the Office of Production Management will clear an award." The Willys award amounted to $11,979,800 for the jeeps and $1,432,064.40 for parts, or a total of $13,411,864.40. Approval of Robert P. Patterson, Under Secretary of War, was dated 31 July 1941.[80]

Holabird was notified of the award on 1 August[81] and a Preference Rating Certificate issued 4 August, which was amended the following month to show an increase in the number of jeeps to be made by Willys to 18,600[82]. The added quantity of 2,600 jeeps secured under the terms of the option in the contract caused the delivery completion date, originally set at 31 December, to be extended to 18 January 1942. Strikes around October at the Midland Steel Products Company, the Mather Spring Company, and current difficulties at Spicer, all of them subcontractors for Willys, were seen as probably having considerable effect upon Willys' future deliveries.[83]

Congressional Investigations into the Jeep Contracts

When Willys ran off with the contract for 16,000 jeeps in July 1941 by underbidding both Ford and American Bantam in open, competitive bidding, for all practical purposes the jeep procurement contest should have ended then and there, since it was a foregone conclusion that standardisation would compel the jeep design to be restricted to the Willys model from there on. But neither Ford nor Bantam was willing to concede defeat as yet. Both continued to try for re-entry into the jeep programme through 1941—in Bantam's case well into 1942—with one notable difference in result: Ford was successful, Bantam was not.

It is interesting to note that the very forces which resulted in Bantam being dropped entirely later enabled Ford to snatch a rather substantial, if partial, victory from the jaws of the defeat it had suffered at the hands of Willys. Events of the day were multiplying rapidly. Within three months after Willys' victory, the Japanese tidal wave at Pearl Harbour was to engulf the entire nation into war. Aided by the Quartermaster Corps, which even after the forcing of the jeep award to Willys by the OPM, had never given up on its plan to utilize Ford's tremendous resources and facilities, Ford was soon to be rushed into production of jeeps based upon Willys design. The interests of national defence as evidenced by the ever increasing requirements for the jeep demanded this move. While Ford was able to accomplish the necessary tooling and machinery conversion to make the Willys jeep and was able to work out its own plan for breaking the universal joint and transfer case bottleneck, Bantam was never able subsequently to demonstrate to the QMC's satisfaction that it could develop a similar programme.

After Ford swung into production alongside Willys, the facilities of the two were deemed by the QMC to be more than sufficient to handle all future jeep requirements, and Bantam never again was able to gain a foothold for itself insofar as the making of jeeps was concerned. Following Pearl Harbour, it did receive war contracts—but not for the manufacture of the jeep. As one of the early "small business" casualties of the war, therefore the case of Bantam received considerable attention from the members of the Truman Committee when that body met in August 1941 and began to take testimony in connection with its investigations of the jeep controversy.

The Truman Committee, organised early in 1941 pursuant to a Senate resolution authorising and directing an investigation of the national defence programme,[84] had been devoting much of its time to defence contracts, interesting itself in such matters as the methods employed for the selection of contractors, the geographic distribution of contracts, and the granting of Government business to small firms. Its work in this regard was representative of the sympathetic concern felt in Congress over the predicament of small business as a result of intensified defence procurement by the Government.

Previous reports and hearings had disclosed to Congress that of $13,000,000,000 worth of defence contracts of $10,000 or more, awarded by the War and Navy Departments from 1 June 1940 through to 28 February 1941, approximately forty-five per cent had been given to six "closely interrelated corporate groups." Chester C. Davis, member of the National Defence Commission, had reported that of $11\frac{1}{2}$ billion dollars worth of prime contracts awarded between 13 June 1940 and 15 February 1941, a total of eighty per cent had been given to sixty-two companies or interconnected groups of companies. Between twenty and twenty-five per cent alone had been absorbed by two groups of concerns having interlocking ownership. According to Senator James E. Murray of Montana, a leading advocate for the protection of the small businessman, statistics for about this time indicated that approximately ninety per cent of small business firms were ending up in failure or liquidation.[85] Among the specific cases involving Quartermaster Corps and War Department procurement and contract policies which were brought to the attention of the Truman Committee as examples of small business in distress, that of the American Bantam Company naturally came to the fore.

Some of the testimony of Bantam's president, Francis H. Fenn, as well as that of Lt. Col. Edwin S. Van Deusen, representing the QMC Motor Transport Division at the hearings, has already been presented in connection with the development and earlier procurement of the jeep. It remains to give the findings and opinions of the Committee as expressed by the chairman, Senator Truman, and Senators Mead and Brewster, members of the investigating body. In conducting its enquiry on the "small business" angle, the Committee centred its examination of the witnesses mostly around the reasons behind the shifts in War Department policy on the procurement of the jeep—from a single source in the beginning which the using arms for the time were content should remain American Bantam, to the three sources of Bantam, Ford, and Willys, and then back once more to one source, which the Quartermaster Corps wanted to be the Ford Motor Company. The Truman Committee found this last change rather puzzling, since the policy of one source seemed to be in direct conflict with another departmental policy—contract distribution—which the War Department was then attempting to carry out through all of its procuring agencies, including the Quartermaster Corps. This policy of contract distribution was supposed to aid small business and distressed communities through the spreading or splitting of War Department contracts wherever possible—in effect a system of multiple sources of supply.

The way to this wider dispersal of defence orders had been thrown open by the act of 2 July 1940, permitting negotiation of defence contracts. Curiously enough, in the procurement of motor vehicles it was also possible for this act to have an opposite effect in that by permitting the elimination of the former principle of competitive bidding between two or more automotive concerns, standardisation could be accomplished under the provisions of the act by the selection of different manufacturers' models in the various weight classifications. This in turn would result in the concentration of motor production to even a greater degree than in the past, instead of distributing it more widely. The directives of the War Department and the action of the Quartermaster Corps on the procurement of the 16,000 jeeps showed that the course of motor procurement policy was now definitely set in the direction of standardisation. The Truman enquiry into the case of the American Bantam Company disclosed that in the inevitable clash between the two War Department policies of standardisation and contract distribution, the latter policy was to be the loser.[86]

The first witness called to the stand before the Truman Committee was Francis H. Fenn, president of Bantam. His testimony in regard to the distribution of the jeep contract and the policy of standardisation indicated that ever since the policy of multiple sources of supply for the jeep was decided upon by the Quartermaster Corps, General Staff, and National Defence Commission in connection with the procurement of the 4,500 quota in 1940, the American Bantam Company had understood and accepted the fact that "the business of any one supplier supplying all the cars was out. That more than one supplier would be needed . . ." According to Fenn, Bantam was "willing to go along and co-operate on any basis. Particularly as the originators of this unit, we most emphatically wanted to stay in . . ." Bantam had also "expected and accepted the theory of standardisation . . . Our company has never questioned the wisdom of it . . . We expected that the best things in each car would be preserved to the Government, and we worked to that end and received excellent co-operation from the Quartermaster Corps all the way down the line in the development of this unit—not only co-operation but courtesy." Bantam thought that standardisation of the jeep "could have been attained and accomplished by round-table conferences that would have given the Government everything good in every car . . . In other words, to take the best frame, to take the best engine, and build a standardised unit."

But what Bantam had not expected to receive was the "schoolboy short cut" in the accomplishment of standardisation. The letting of the bids for the 16,000 jeeps on an "all or none" basis and on a set of specifications involving changes desired by the Army which it was thought only Ford could make without undue hardship, "came as an extreme shock" to Bantam which until then had not even remotely realised "that it was going to be an all-or-none proposition . . . We were simply caught, that's all."

After the Committee had enquired into Bantam's financial status, its loans from the RFC, and the labour conditions in Butler, Pennsylvania, Senator Brewster said:

> Your picture is, then, that your facilities and much of your personnel may be dissipated if the War Department follows a different policy.
> *Mr. Fenn.* If the policy is changed to one manufacturer, all these men will be out of work.
> *Senator Brewster.* And I assume from the national standpoint there are some advantages in not too great concentrations locally of our production.
> *Mr. Fenn.* I would say so.
> *Senator Brewster.* And also we have been hearing something about small concerns, haven't we, getting a little business?
> *Mr. Fenn.* Well, there was a meeting in New York about that this week or last week, if I remember. We are not very large, but we have been awfully sincere and honest in producing this car.
> *The Chairman.* It is your baby, isn't it?
> *Mr. Fenn.* It is our baby, and building the first one in 49 days meant day and night for about 12 or 15 of us . . .[87]

Succeeding Fenn on the witness stand was Lt. Col. Edwin S. Van Deusen, chief of the procurement branch of the Motor Transport Division. The history of the development and first procurements of the jeep up to the last award for 16,000 was reviewed by Colonel Van Deusen and the Committee, including the questions of the increases in the weight specifications, the different points of view between the Quartermaster Corps and the using arms, the disagreement over the procurement of the first 4,500 jeeps, the weight of the Willys pilot model, and the delivery schedules of each of the three manufacturers. Colonel Van Deusen's testimony on these matters, some of which has already been cited, was substantially in accord with the account of the jeep as presented in this monograph up to this point. The reasons for the changing policies of the War Department in regard to the procurement of the jeep, all of them unfavourable to the Bantam Company, were then discussed by the Committee and Van Deusen.

Senator Brewster wished to know whether the directives of the General Staff and the Under Secretary of War on the procurement of the 16,000 jeeps was any reversal in Quartermaster policy "from your original idea of distribution." Van Deusen answered, "No," and the following colloquy then ensued:

Senator Brewster. Well, I thought you wanted three sources.

Colonel Van Deusen. We wanted three sources in connection with the development and service test of these to determine what a suitable vehicle would be and whether any one of the three manufacturers would build a suitable vehicle.

Senator Mead. And then, Colonel, once you established what was a suitable model, it would be very easy for you to standardise it, and once it was standardised, it would be easy for the three plants to produce them according to your standardised specification. So why determine to eliminate two in favour of one plant when the need is so great and so instant?

Colonel Van Deusen. That is true where you are building and buying to a design. We are not building and buying to a design. We are buying commercially produced units.

Senator Mead. Yes; but why wouldn't you standardise them? You were looking for a model that would meet with your specifications, your tests. Why couldn't you standardise them and why couldn't you, as long as you needed them, thousands of them, allow a pioneering company already in the field to participate in the production of this standardised model?

Colonel Van Deusen. We could standardise if we were to specify the engine will be Continental, model so-and-so, the transfer case and transmission shall be Spicer or Warner's, model so-and-so, the axle shall be Timken or Spicer, model so-and-so.

Senator Mead. Or equivalent, or something of that sort.

Colonel Van Deusen. If you put the word "or equal" in there, you can't force the procurement of the type to secure the standardisation. There is only one way of attaining complete standardisation, and that is to draw on the board the item in complete detail and force everybody to make that item. When you are buying commercial items, there is a different combination by different manufacturers, any one of which may meet the specification and give you a satisfactory vehicle.

Senator Mead. So that on one occasion we have the Assistant Secretary up here and he tells us that under his directives he won't allow any loans for plant expansion or for the purpose of new machines if there is plant and machines already available for a given contract.

Colonel Van Deusen. That is true, and that is one of the points that I want to bring out.

Senator Mead. There are so many things true that one can't understand the truisms of all of them when one tries to fit them together.

Now, we have another witness who tells us—and this is evidently true, too—that in order to get a certain design it is absolutely necessary to put one company completely out of business, with its plant, its machinery, and its skilled workers, and allow another company which has been enjoying the inertia of bankruptcy, and with cobwebs and rust around the plant and machines, to go to the Government and get a loan of $3,000,000, so that the Government actually is going into the business of putting a pioneering company completely out of business.

The Chairman. One that it financed itself.

Senator Mead. And that is the policy of the War Department, which just a few days ago came before this committee and said, "Oh, we spread all the contracts." I wonder whether it is spreading the contracts or spreading something else that is actually being done in reality.

Colonel Van Deusen. I have no comment to make on that.

Senator Mead. Colonel, this isn't meant for criticism of you or your work. You are just a cog in a machine, and you are doing your bit.

The Chairman. We are criticising policy. It is a very evident one.
Senator Mead. It is a policy that really merits strong criticism . . .

Senator Mead then began to read aloud with several interpolations of his own, from a letter he said was signed by the Chief of Cavalry. This communication, as read by Senator Mead, was an indictment of the entire procedure and manner by which the jeep development and procurement had been handled. It declared that too many people have had "a finger in the Bantam pie", and that at one time or another everyone from the US Senate down to the humblest clerk had made some decision in connection with the jeep. Despite the fact that work on the Bantam development had been started in 1940, time was still being wasted in waiting for a field test of the 4,500 vehicles, and the training of cavalry units had been seriously hampered. At about the time this letter was written, the issue of jeeps to the using arms was said currently to be 57, with 74 expected to be issued during June and July and a possible 213 in September. After finishing quoting from this letter, Senator Mead said: "I want to tell you, if Joe Stalin doesn't stall that fellow Adolf over there in the snows of Russia, we will be short a few 'jeeps' when the time comes.

"I want to tell you this isn't a Congressman that is criticising. This isn't the Bantam Car Co. looking for an adjustment of a grievance. This letter is signed by the Major General of the United States, Chief of Cavalry, and I think it should be considered by the Department; and it is high time that we got every plant that can make 'jeeps' under full mass-production order."

To this, Colonel Van Deusen answered: "If that letter was signed by General Herr, he is not acquainted with some of the facts in the case." He then proceeded to show that in spite of strikes, Ford had completed its delivery of 1,500 jeeps, except for two, by 19 May 1941.

In reply to a final question by Senator Truman as to which of the three jeeps he thought the best, Colonel Van Deusen answered, "Any one of the three will do the job."[88]

One week later John D. Biggers, Director of Production, OPM, appeared before the Truman Committee to tell of his part in the jeep affair. He denied that he had influenced the award to Willys, or that Bantam had lost out because it had had a fight with OPM. In fact, Biggers didn't "blame them [Bantam] for feeling badly [sic] about it, because they did quite an important pioneering job . . ."[89]

In respect to the distribution of contracts, Biggers more than once in his testimony drew the attention of the committee to the fact that both Mr. Knudsen and he had held out for the multiple source of supply idea from the start. He pointed out that when the question first came up the year before in connection with the proposed purchase of 1,500 jeeps, the Defence Committee had backed up the viewpoint of the Quartermaster Corps which was then voting for more than one source.[90]

Biggers told the Committee that even after the Quartermaster Corps changed its mind early in 1941, claiming that the need for standardisation and simplification of field maintenance made it imperative that all future orders for trucks in every category should be awarded, through negotiation, to the then current suppliers of the vehicles provided their equipment had proven satisfactory,[91] Knudsen and he had taken the position that this policy was not wise and that a second source of supply should be set up for each vehicle.

In the jeep situation, particularly, it would have been Biggers' preference to have kept Bantam in the programme. A satisfactory solution to the standardisation problem could have been found, he felt, through the design of a standard vehicle. On this point, as revealed by the following concluding testimony, both Senator Truman and Biggers were in complete agreement:

The Chairman. What impressed us was that you had been very careful to divide the first 1,500 three ways, and we couldn't see why the 16,000 couldn't be divided the same way so as to keep the Bantam Co. running, since they had done all the pioneering in the beginning to make the car available for Army use.

Mr. Biggers. Mr. Chairman, that would have been my preference.

The Chairman. It seems to me that is what should have been done.

Mr. Biggers. My preference would have been that the Army take time to design a standard vehicle and let two or more of these companies continue to supply it. They said that time didn't permit and that the bid method was chosen and the contract was awarded to the low bidder. I had no part in recommending the award, but I think that Mr. Knudsen's judgement as to the competence of an automobile company to make 16,000 vehicles is certainly dependable judgement.

The Chairman. I wouldn't doubt that . . .

Beside the Truman Committee, the House Military Affairs Committee, through a subcommittee headed by Congressman Faddis, also took a hand in investigating the jeep contracts. Like the Senate group, it apparently was also interested in the matter from the standpoint of distribution of war orders to small business. On 10 October 1941, Mr. Julius H. Amberg, Special Assistant to the Secretary of War, wrote a memorandum to Colonels Van Deusen and Dow apprising them of the forthcoming House inquiry. Mr. Amberg indicated that the "chief attack" of the subcommittee might be directed against the OPM Labour Division which the counsel for the Military Affairs Committee, Mr. Perry, seemed "to think influenced the decision in favour of Willys-Overland, although so far as you and I saw directly, the decision was made by Messrs. Knudsen, Biggers and Nelson." Van Deusen and Dow were advised to have ready all data on the case in the event that either or both of them were called to testify. Information was requeted as to what Willys' final delivery schedule was to be as well as the opinions of Van Deusen and Dow as to Willys' chances of completing delivery on time.[92]

The requested information was promptly sent to Mr. Amberg by Colonel Van Deusen. Deliveries on the order for the 16,000 jeeps, originally set to start on 8 November 1941, and end not later than 31 December 1941, had now been revised because of the increase in the order to 18,600 through the exercise of the option secured at the time of the original award. Willys was now expected to start delivery on 27 October and complete the order by 18 January of the following year. As to whether Willys would be able to fulfil this schedule, Colonel Van Deusen wrote: "The full effect of the recent strike at Midland Steel Products Company, Mather Spring Company and current difficulties in Spicer Manufacturing Corporation, current supplier to Willys-Overland Incorporated are not yet known, but undoubtedly will affect the actual deliveries to take place from the Willys-Overland plant."[93]

The interim general report of the House Military Affairs Committee, published the following June, briefly reviewed the history of the jeep controversy but did not commit the Committee to any definite stand on the matter as had been taken by members of the Truman group at their hearings. The report noted that while Willys had underbid Ford by six dollars and Bantam by forty dollars on the procurement of the 16,000 jeeps, the War Department had wished to negotiate the entire contract with Ford, since it "felt that Ford could be relied upon with greater assurance to deliver their cars on time; that although all three companies got their axles from Spicer in Toledo, Ford was in a better position to receive priority because of quantities regularly purchased . . . that Ford would be able to proceed with little tooling up while in the instance of Willys-Overland a considerable amount was needed with resultant delays; that Bantam was entirely an assembly plant; that Ford did not require Government financing but Willys-Overland, in receivership for five years, required complete financing, undoubtedly through the Reconstruction Finance Corporation, this no doubt also obtained in the case of Bantam."

Included in the report was a statement that two representatives of the CIO United Automobile Workers' Union, accompanied by an OPM man, were sent by Willys to see Mr. Amberg on 14 July 1941, to argue that the award should be made to Willys pursuant to its low bid, since "it would furnish work in Toledo, where it was greatly needed," but that this contingent apparently had no success whatever in "altering the opinion of the War Department as to the advisability of awarding the contract to Ford."

The report also took note of Bantam's contention that as the jeep development had been "very definitely the result of their own effort," recognition of this fact by the Government should have been accorded them by the award of at least part of the order. Entered also was the War Department's denial of Bantam's charge that the specifications had been so drawn as to eliminate all from bidding except Ford.

In connection with Bantam's last order for 1,000 of the 1/4-tons, the report said: "They could have been delivered on schedule but the maker was requested to slow down on production. The reason given by the War Department was their desire to defer delivery until after Army manoeuvres in order to determine their value." In respect to Willys' ability to comply with the delivery terms of the contract for the 16,000 jeeps, the report contained the statement: "It was seriously questioned whether Willys-Overland was in a position to comply with the terms of the contract to produce 16,000 of such cars by May 1942, beginning deliveries in October 1941, as that would mean 400 cars a day."[94]

Re-entry of Ford into the Jeep Programme

While the decision of the OPM forcing the award of the contract for the 16,000 jeeps to Willys in July 1941, instead of to Ford where the QMC wished to place it, was a definite setback to the plan to utilise Ford's great production facilities for the jeep, it proved to be only a temporary one. With war within a few months a distinct possibility at the time, the probable vast increase in jeep requirements that would be necessary in the event it did occur, together with the probability that Willys alone would not be able to meet the requirements, conspired to put Ford back into the jeep production programme by October, with all of the additional tooling facilities the Quartermaster Corps considered vital to the breaking of the production bottlenecks it foresaw in such a contingency. The one obstacle to putting Ford into production that at first seemed insurmountable when efforts in this direction were made in August, was the matter of standardisation. With standardisation already virtually assured by the award of the contract for the entire 16,000 jeeps to Willys, this all-important feature would have to be cast overboard if Ford again was to be permitted to manufacture 1/4-tons of its own design. Since the War Department by virtue of the General Staff directive of 8 July to the Under Secretary of War now seemed definitely committed to this principle, the Quartermaster Corps was hardly in a position to propose its overthrow, especially since it had lately been an advocate of standardisation itself. Yet in the OQMG Motor Transport Division it seemed to some that the advantages to be gained from Ford production would more than offset the loss of standardisation.

The question came up for discussion as a result of a letter sent by Ford to Motor Transport almost immediately after Ford learned that the contract award had been made to Willys. In this letter Ford called attention to the option provision in the invitation whereby "at the discretion of the Army" the initial quantity of 16,000 jeeps to be purchased could be increased by fifty per cent. Ford submitted that the best interests of national defence would be served by the award of a contract for this 8,000 increase to the Ford Motor Company. Should this award be given to Ford, the company asserted that it would provide entirely separate tooling for the production of the axles, constant velocity joints, transfer cases, drive shafts, and drive shaft universal joints, thus liquidating in advance any possibility of bottlenecks developing among these items. The capacity of suppliers of other parts to Ford, such as frames, wheels, fuel tanks, fuel filters, and brakes, had been thoroughly investigated and found to be ample. Furthermore, the "far reaching facilities" of Ford would give assurance of supply of critical raw materials such as pig iron, steel, glass, and other items.

The net result of all this would be to "give the Army an unquestioned volume source of supply entirely independent of the original contract, thus providing adequate insurance against any production contingency that might arise." Prices per truck and for spare parts were to be the same as in Ford's original bid for the 16,000 ¼-tons, with delivery completed by 26 January 1942, provided the award was received not later than 15 August 1941.[95]

Ford's proposal was regarded favourably by Motor Transport's purchasing and contracting officer, Lieutenant Colonel Ingram. In a memorandum to Colonel Van Deusen, Chief of Motor Transport's Procurement Branch, Ingram declared that should the Army's jeep requirements increase considerably, he considered that the addition of Ford's large production capacity, separate tooling facilities, and sources for raw materials, would be distinctly advantageous in meeting these requirements, if they should prove beyond the capacity of Willys. In respect of the loss of standardisation which would result from having two makes of jeeps, he pointed out that the Army already had in service 4,500 ¼-tons built by Ford, Willys, and Bantam, with another 1,000 each on order with Bantam and Ford. It was Ingram's opinion that the advantages to be gained by the inclusion of Ford in the jeep programme appeared to outweigh the loss of standardisation and that, therefore, it would be a "smart move on the part of the Army to make this award to the Ford Motor Company."[96]

But the viewpoint of the Chief of the Contract Control Branch, when consulted on this question, was that while the comments of Colonel Ingram were "properly for consideration," many of them had already been offered in support of the QMC's original proposal to award the entire contract to Ford. Also, Motor Transport was in no position to make an award for 8,000 additional jeeps until money was available, since it

had only been authorised to purchase $14,000,000 worth of jeeps. Hence it was the recommendation of the Contract Control Branch that the last directive of the Adjutant General be carried out without change and that when additional funds were provided, a review of the situation should be made as to the progress of Willys to "see if we have a better case to present."[97]

After the subject of the Ford proposal had been discussed between Colonel Van Deusen and the Chief of the Motor Transport Division, General Barzynski, the latter decided that inasmuch as the contract for the 16,000 ¼-tons had already been completed with Willys, including the option for additional vehicles, it did not appear reasonable to enter into negotiations with Ford under the "pretext" that Willys-Overland could not comply with its contract, unless by its subsequent performance it clearly demonstrated that it was unable to do so. Therefore, no action should be undertaken with the Ford Motor Company for the supply of jeeps to the United States Army. However, if a concurrent need for jeeps arose in connection with defence aid (lend-lease), that would be another question to be decided separately.[98]

Efforts to further the plan for the inclusion of Ford in the jeep production programme were given sharp impetus in October, assuring success, when at the request of the Motor Transport contracting officer at Holabird, Wardon Canady, Chairman of the Board of Willys, outlined a plan by which Willys agreed to co-operate in the establishment of a second entirely independent source for the production of ¼-tons in accordance with the Willys design. In the event that the War Department did decide to standardise on the Willys jeep, Willys agreed to furnish any designated manufacturer full and complete information necessary to produce identical vehicles, including Van Dyke drawings, bills of material, material and heat treating specifications, parts lists, etc. The United States or any manufacturer named by it would be given a complete list and details of patents, royalties, patent agreements, and licence agreements affecting the manufacture of these vehicles. Willys would give to the Government an irrevocable non-exclusive licence, without payment of royalties, to make, have made, use, maintain, and dispose of all devices embodying inventions covered by patents owned or controlled by Willys-Overland Motors, Incorporated, necessary to the production of the Willys jeep. Express conditions to this were that these licences were to extend only to the making of jeeps for the United States Government, and that the granting of any licence under patents was to be subject to the approval of the Reconstruction Finance Corporation.

In consideration of the above, it was to be mutually agreed that Willys would continue to be given contracts to manufacture jeeps in accordance with its productive ability, the delivery requirements of the Government, and the maintenance of production at both sources. Willys also was to be given the same consideration as the alternate source in remuneration for special tooling and was to be paid a price for its product comparable to that paid the alternate source.[99]

Action to put this agreement into effect was swift. A letter of intent to purchase 15,000 instead of 8,000 jeeps from Ford, to be built to the Willys design, was forwarded by the Quartermaster General to the Under Secretary of War on 14 October[100] and approved by that official on the same day, with the provision that the letter was not to be released until written clearance had been obtained from the Office of Production Management.[101] The OPM, through its Director of Purchases approved the proposal on 16 October.[102] Request for permission for Willys to execute licences under patents was made to the RFC Board of Directors at about the same time.[103] On 16 October the OQMG Public Relations Branch announced: "Ford and Willys to Make Identical Jeeps,"[104] and the War Department made a similar announcement, terming it the first arrangement of its kind since the First World War.[105] A copy of the Willys agreement was sent the Ford Motor Company at Alexandria, Virginia, on 21 October (presumably to other Ford branches as well),[106] and on 10 November, Willys was officially advised by Colonel Ingram that in accordance with the provisions embodied in Willys' proposal of 10 October, the Office of the Quartermaster General was now designating the Ford Motor Company as the alternate source to which Willys was to furnish all of the necessary information called for by its agreement.[107]

While the long campaign of the Quartermaster Corps and the Ford Motor Company to bring Ford into production of the jeep, dating back to 1940, may be considered to have ended, for all practical purposes, with the approval of the October letter of intent, it was not until the following January that the contract for the 15,000 jeeps was finally cleared. In the meantime Pearl Harbour had occurred and the country was at war. Arrangements to bring part of the immense resources and facilities of the Ford Motor Company into the Quartermaster fold for the making of jeeps apparently had been concluded in the nick of time.

The negotiated contract approved of by the Under Secretary of War on 10 January 1942,[108] was for a total consideration of $14,623,900, broken down as follows:

Quantity	FOB Point	Net Unit Cost $	Total $
3,500	Dearborn, Mich.	951.76	3,331,160
2,500	Chester, Pa.	976.76	2,441,900
2,500	Dallas, Tex.	986.76	2,466,900
4,000	Louisville, Ky.	966.76	3,867,040
2,500	Long Beach, Calif.	1,006.76	2,516,900
15,000			14,623,900

Taken into consideration by the above net prices was the usual Ford discount of fifty dollars per vehicle for payment within thirty days. Also included were an additional charge of $140 per vehicle for tooling costs; a charge of $46.16 to cover overtime work necessary to complete delivery by 31 March 1942; and a further charge of $.79 for purchasing of joints to anticipate Ford tooling.[109] These net prices represented a considerable increase over Ford's previous quotation of $782.59 per unit in its bid on the 16,000 jeeps in 1941 when the competitive bidding system was employed, totalling over $2,000,000 more for the 15,000 jeeps than Ford's previous offer on the entire lot of 16,000. While tooling costs had also been included in Ford's proposal of 6 August 1941, when it offered to build 8,000 jeeps at the same price it had quoted in its previous bidding against Willys and Bantam, that offer was based on jeeps of Ford design and did not contemplate making Willys models.[110]

Vehicle changes in the jeep, which was being modified and improved from time to time, caused the granting of authority for the issuance of a change order on Ford's contract in the total amount of $384,600. While no change in the delivery time was anticipated, the requested modifications caused the weight of the jeep to be increased by eighty-two pounds.[111] By 24 March 1942, delivery was slightly behind schedule, and permission was granted Ford to transfer some of the production originally scheduled for Louisville, to the Ford River Rouge plant at Dearborn in order to complete production at all branches in approximately the same time, early in April.[112]

A most important condition was included in the approval of the Ford contract by the Office of the Under Secretary of War, by which ownership of all of the tooling equipment such as dies, jigs, and fixtures purchased by Ford under the allowance of $140 per jeep, for "tooling costs," totalling $2,100,000, was to vest in the Government. This was the first time since the national defence effort had been under way that the Government sought to take title, as the rightful owner, to automotive equipment for which it was footing the bill. Ultimately many other "contract control" measures designed to check on profits and costs were to be instituted, but at the time the Ford contract was under consideration, the idea that the Government would own the tools it had paid for and would have the right to dictate their eventual disposition, was still sufficiently novel within the Quartermaster Corps Motor Transport Division to cause it to see in such a ruling the development of complications and difficulties in past as well as future procurements. Yet ever since the Ford letter of intent of 4 October 1941, the Office of Production Management had clearly indicated that it was determined to press this matter of Government ownership of tools to a conclusion.

At that time, Hiram S. Brown, Assistant Director of Purchases, OPM, wrote the Quartermaster General: "A careful reading of your proposed letter of intent to the Ford Motor Company . . . does not specifically state that the $2,100,000 of tools will be owned by the United States Government and that the contract with the Ford Motor Company will contain the usual provisions for government protection in such ownership." As the letter of intent definitely provided for the reimbursement of Ford for the full cost of tooling, Brown said that the OPM was assuming that upon such payment the Government would become the owner of the tools. Since the Quartermaster General in a telephone conversation with Mr. Brown had assured the latter that all necessary steps would be taken to protect the Government's interest in the tools, a written confirmation on this point was requested by OPM for the record.[113]

Both the purchasing and contracting officer and executive assistant of Motor Transport voiced objections to this proposal in similar memoranda to Motor Transport's Acting Chief, Colonel Lawes. The purchasing and contracting officer pointed out that previous letters of intent requiring tooling expenditures issued under date of 28 March 1941, to such corporations as General Motors, International Harvester, Mack, Fruehauf Trailers, and Gar Wood, had not included such a provision. In the letter of intent sent the Spicer Manufacturing Corporation on 7 November 1940, for the manufacture of axles, transfer cases, and propeller shafts, including the tooling necessary to produce these items, no mention of Government ownership of tools had been made. The same was true of the letter of intent to the Warner Gear Division of Borg-Warner Corporation, dated 17 February 1941. In this letter, however, the Government had reserved "control" of the use of tooling.

The contracting office argued that the producing of dies, jigs, and fixtures comprising most of the tooling would have no value to the Government if divorced from the machines. Also, since much of the tooling only involved conversion of machines already owned by the companies, tooling costs resolved themselves largely into labour costs, rather than tangible objects to which ownership could be claimed. Furthermore, if the Army took title to the dies, jigs, and fixtures, the rules of the Government would necessitate the setting up of a property accounting procedure for such tools as well as frequent checking to see that they were being conserved properly. The Government would have to replace all worn-out tools whereas if the ownership remained with the contractor, replacement would be his responsibility without additional cost to the Government.

As the Ford letter already contained a provision that all tools paid for by the Government would "be used exclusively for the production of trucks manufactured or to be manufactured for the War Department" unless the contracting officer authorised other uses for them, it was contended further that the Army already had complete control of the use of the tools for its own purpose. The reason given for permitting the contracting officer to authorise "production of trucks manufactured for other than the War Department," was that this would permit the retention of authority by the War Department to allow Ford to build trucks for other countries with these tools, when properly authorised to do so.[114]

The executive assistant of Motor Transport advanced reasons similar to the above. In addition he noted that as the letter of intent definitely committed Ford to the tooling programme at a cost of not more than $2,100,000, Ford would have to go through with it without further compensation even if it turned out that the tooling cost twice as much. Again, since Ford would have to pay many of its subcontractors for tooling, the cost of checking and recording all of this would be prohibitive. Government ownership of dies, jigs, patterns, and fixtures, would also mean Government responsibility for storage, maintenance, and replacement of tools, much of which would be of no use to other contractors because of the different machines used. The executive assistant believed, however, that when the final contract was negotiated it would be advisable to write off the tooling against the order with a credit to the Government for any "salvage value," and that after the contract had been completed, if the Government wished to place the next order with some other contractor, the Ford Company would agree to turn over all tools that could be profitably employed by the new maker, in whatever condition they might be at the conclusion of the present Ford contract.[115]

The opinions of the two Motor Transport executives were forwarded to the Quartermaster General by Colonel Lawes together with a suggested reply to Colonel Brown which the Quartermaster General was asked to note did not "commit the Quartermaster Corps to the proposition that the tools must become the property of the Government." The proposed answer to Colonel Brown simply stated that the proper steps would "be taken at the time the contract is entered into with this company to adequately protect the Government's interest in these tools." Lawes advised the Quartermaster General that considerable study ought to be given this matter before committing the OQMG to any definite course of action, since it appeared that Colonel Brown's thought was that the Government must own the tools, not only on the Ford contract but in all future cases. Past contracts were to be reviewed to this same end. Ordnance contracts, as well as Quartermaster, were to be investigated in connection with Government ownership of tools, and Colonel Lawes believed Brown intended "to bring up the whole question of government ownership of tools and seek a decision which may complicate, not only our future but also our past contract procurements."[116]

Nevertheless, the Office of Production Management was successful in getting through the policy it advocated, for on 14 November 1941, Colonel Brown was notified by the Quartermaster General that the formal contract with Ford would incorporate a stipulation "that all special dies, jigs, fixtures and other tools to be acquired for the production of these vehicles would become the property of the United States."[117]

Even before the approval of the final contract for 15,000 jeeps with Ford, negotiated a month after Pearl Harbour, both Ford and Willys were beginning to receive tremendous additional orders for jeeps. Letters of intent dated 29 December 1941, were sent to both concerns, Ford's letter calling for 63,146 jeeps[118] and Willys' for 43,601.[119] The quantity allotted to Ford was then increased to 85,546,[120] and Willys' amount was likewise raised to 61,794.[121] From this point on, Army and lend-lease requirements for the jeep began to run into the hundred of thousands.

By August 1942, the policy of the Quartermaster General's Office in respect to dividing future jeep contracts between Ford and Willys, was to award contracts to both "for such number of vehicles as, when added to the entire commitments from the outset to Ford and Willys in the past, will leave Ford and Willys in an exactly fifty-fifty position over the entire period." Computation of these quantities was not to take into consideration contracts for the amphibian counterpart of the jeep which Ford was then preparing to produce for the Army. The amphibian jeeps were to be regarded as extra vehicles to Ford, and Willys was not to be concerned with such production.[122]

Failure of American Bantam to Regain Entry into the Jeep Programme

The re-entry of Ford into the ¼-ton production programme, plus the subsequent orders to Willys and Ford for almost 150,000 jeeps, sealed the fate of the American Bantam Company for the duration of the war, insofar as the making of these vehicles was concerned. The elimination of Bantam from the jeep manufacturing programme had, by 1942, become almost a dead certainty. There were two principal obstacles placed before Bantam in its campaign to secure a share of future jeep contracts which proved impossible for that concern to hurdle.

First, Bantam was never able to demonstrate to the Quartermaster Corps' satisfaction, as Ford had done, a plan for the production of the standardised Willys model that would provide additional sources for production of bottleneck items without further strain on the already critical machine tool industry. The new and separate set of facilities provided by Ford for producing the axle and joint bottleneck items for the jeep, tooled entirely by itself, meant that the entire output of Spicer on these items could now flow to the Willys assembly line. The Quartermaster Corps and the War Department could see little point in diverting any of this production or rendering any other assistance in the way of critical machine tool priorities, merely to put Bantam back into the jeep business.

Even if, by some chance, Bantam had been able to overcome this production barrier unassisted, it would still have been confronted by a second hurdle that was certain to prove insurmountable: the accomplished fact of Ford and Willys production. For by 1942 it was plainly evident that the combined productive capacity of Willys and Ford was going to be more than sufficient to handle all future Army and lend-lease requirements for the jeep.

Against these two handicaps, the arguments of Bantam and its proponents availed little. The country was at war, and in view of the exigency of the jeep situation the QMC undoubtedly felt that it was scarcely in a position to give consideration to such a matter as the avowed War Department policy of favouring small business or the contention of Bantam that, as the collaborator with Spicer in the development of that concern's machine tool facilities, it was rightfully entitled to its share of Spicer's prodution. Nevertheless, between the time of the award of the 16,000 jeeps to Willys in July 1941, and its final plea to General Brehon B. Somervell, Commanding General of the Army's Services of Supply, in March 1942, the American Bantam

Company put up a strenuous, if losing, battle to get back into the jeep picture. Eventually, it had to be content with the lesser consolation of sharing with Willys contracts for two-wheel trailers for the jeep.

In addition to presenting its case before the Truman Committee in August 1941, Bantam enlisted the aid of Senator Joseph S. Guffey of Pennsylvania. Replying to a letter the Senator had written on 20 October suggesting that Bantam be assigned a fair portion of the 15,000 jeep order which had just been given to Ford, the Quartermaster General said, "we should like to consider additional orders for this company for the reasons expressed in your letter, as well as the War Department policy of favouring small companies. Our co-operation with the American Bantam Car Company has been shown in the past by the orders enumerated in your letter." But when the development of the jeep was first being considered, one of the initial instructions to the Quartermaster Corps had been to consider sources of supply "not only in the light of the finished vehicles' performance as related to military requirements, but equally in terms of facilities for manufacture with consequent delivery possibilities in a minimum amount of time."

"The service tests having been completed," continued the Quartermaster General, "we asked for bids on a large number from all probable manufacturers. The Willys-Overland Company was low bidder and, meeting all requirements, was given the order."

The importance of accomplishing standardisation by freezing the design of the jeep on the first large quantity order was, of course, fully understood by the Senator, the letter said. The Quartermaster General recalled that failure to standardise in the First World War had had a serious effect upon the maintenance and spare parts situation in the field, with much resulting confusion, loss of equipment, damage to combat forces, and unnecessary costs. While the policy of standardising on the Willys design had been accepted by both Ford and Bantam, so far only Ford had been able to present a programme covering the development of an entirely separate set of facilities for production of the critical axle and related items, including tooling for the same. Although Bantam had made statements that the company was prepared to standardise on the approved design, no positive plan had as yet been submitted. The Quartermaster General further pointed out to Senator Guffey that justification for the establishment of a third source for the jeep would depend upon future requirements, "which naturally would have to be shown before I would be justified in approving an expenditure of public funds."

All of this had been discussed with Bantam representatives and was understood by them, the letter said. If any possibility of using the Bantam plant had been overlooked by the Quartermaster Corps, "we shall be pleased to discuss the matter with Bantam officials, and it is possible that more orders will develop in the future in which their facilities may be required." Concluding the letter was the statement: "Our investigation indicates that this order had been handled without any prejudice whatever against the American Bantam Car Company and that the final disposition has been made to the best interest of the Army.[123]

Following this polite but firm rejection of Senator Guffey's suggestion, the Bantam Company apparently sought to meet the OQMG's conditions as to an additional set of production facilities and tooling for same, for on 19 November, another letter from the Quartermaster General to Senator Guffey indicated that the OQMG was still dubious about Bantam as a third source for the manufacture of the jeep. "The proposal of this company," wrote the Quartermaster General, "contains several features which must be analysed as to their possibility of application and effect upon adopted standardisation as well as the production sources involved." There was nothing in Bantam's proposal indicating its ability to secure duplicate sources of supply for the constant velocity universal joints used in the front driving axles, the prize bottleneck in jeep production. The Quartermaster General's Office doubted that Bantam's contemplated source for the constant velocity joints, The Gear Grinding Machine Company, Detroit, could "reasonably be expected to perform in accordance with the letter of 30 October 1941, from that company, without material assistance and additional tooling."

The letter emphasised again "the fact that the utilisation of the American Bantam Car Company as an additional source for the completed vehicles, assuming satisfactory clarification of the questions still pending, can be justified only on the basis of additional requirements... As previously stated, placement of a contract with this company cannot be justified solely by reason of the fact that a third source of these trucks is being developed." Senator Guffey once more was assured that upon clarification of the present incomplete information from Bantam regarding duplicate sources for critical components of the jeep, and "upon the development of a further requirement which, in the opinion of this office, will warrant securing additional productive facilities to meet such requirements," full consideration would be given to Bantam's offer.[124]

However, nothing in the way of an order to Bantam materialised from these negotiations. The shock of Pearl Harbour came and went, and the country buckled down to the difficult job of winning the war. For 1942 the QMC Motor Transport Division was faced with the task of meeting estimated procurement requirements for 958,543 trucks and other vehicles.[125] While not entirely set to meet the full impact of war requirements in the medium and heavy duty field, although production facilities in these categories had been expanded 600% since 1940, Motor Transport and the American automobile industry were well prepared to handle Army and lend-lease requirements in the light truck field.

This was especially true of the ¼-ton programme that had now been built around the enormous combined resources of Ford and Willys. Of the total 1942 requirements of 337,374 four-wheel drive trucks embracing the 1½-ton, ¾-ton, and ¼-ton grops, 179,177 were for jeeps.[126] To meet these requirements there was the combined Ford-Willys production capacity rated at 210,404 jeeps for the year, giving a possible average of more than 31,000 vehicles.[127] An even greater surplus of productive capacity over estimated requirements was foreseen for 1943 when it was figured that the average would be 58,131, even though the procurement requirements for that year called for practically 200,000 jeeps.[128] Hence it can be seen why the combined ability of Ford and Willys to take care of every conceivable demand for jeeps, probably for the entire war, caused the Office of the Quartermaster General to continue to feel that placement of jeep orders with Bantam was "not warranted". This was still the official QMC attitude some months later when the Bantam Company made its appeal to General Somervell for a share in the jeep business. Outside pressure, stemming from the original intense competition between Bantam, Ford and Willys over the earlier jeep contracts, also showed itself at this time. Willys particularly made no secret of its protest over any further division of jeep contracts, claiming it could produce almost twice as many jeeps as it was then being permitted to build.

The letter which was written to General Somervell by Bantam's president, Francis H. Fenn, was dated 23 March 1942. In it Fenn chronologically reviewed the whole history of the jeep from Bantam's point of view and argued vigorously on behalf of the re-entry of Bantam into the jeep programme. He said that late in 1937 he "wrote the War Department suggesting that inasmuch as the Bantam car had been completely revamped, provided with a new and more powerful engine, and other features . . . we, in our opinion, could furnish a light weapons-carrier, which would outperform motorcycles and would perform just about any job required of it." While this correspondence continued intermittently, it was not until June 1940, that any interest was shown in Bantam's car. It was at this time that the Ordnance Committee appeared at Bantam's plant and was given demonstrations of Bantam's performance. "When the demonstrations were completed," wrote Fenn, "the Technical Committee and Bantam people returned to my office, where a sketch of the intended car was drawn up, a photostat of which I am attaching hereto. It was from this rude sketch, together with a general understanding as to the specifications of the car, that we went to work on the development of the vehicle." Fenn stressed the point to General Somervell that at that time there had not existed any axles, transfer cases, universal joints, or other primary components which were to go into the eventual jeep. These were developed in co-operation with the Spicer Company, the first set of axles, for example, having to be hogged out of solid steel.

In connection with Ford and Willys being brought into the programme later on, after Bantam had built and delivered the first seventy models of the jeep, finishing the first pilot in forty-nine days, Fenn said that in fairness to Bantam it should be noted that "before either of the others had received orders, our cars were in Holabird, undergoing tests, and were subjected to the thorough scrutiny of competitive enginers. In brief, although this had been our idea for years, we shortly found ourselves completely out of the picture."

This came about when Willys received the contract for the 16,000 jeeps by underbidding both Ford and Bantam, the latter by forty dollars per jeep. Bantam had no complaint to offer on this score, admitting that "we were beaten and beaten fairly." Although Bantam also had been underbid a few dollars per jeep by Ford on this same invitation, on the matter of parts Ford's bid had been higher, "so that on the complete bid, covering cars and parts, Bantam stood No. 2 on the list." Since then, however, contracts for a quarter of a million jeeps had gone to Ford and Willys on a negotiated basis with both, and at prices ranging from seventy-five to one hundred and twenty-five dollars higher than the price Bantam had originally bid. The 16,000 jeeps bought from Willys was the only quantity ever procured at the low price of Willys' bid. Since then the negotiated prices had risen steadily and now were far beyond that original price of $748. It was Fenn's contention, therefore, that Bantam should have been given the opportunity to negotiate for some of this jeep business along with Ford and Willys.

Fenn declared that Bantam had paid Spicer over $130,000 for the purpose of tooling axles, transfer cases, and universal joints, in the expectancy that this would provide Bantam with fifty to one hundred sets of axles per day, and "inasmuch as we paid this money and worked in the development and engineering of these units, we cannot understand why the capacity has been taken from us . . ." Although he had been in business for many years, Fenn stated that he knew "of no case in the history of modern business which parallels this one."

In respect of standardisation, Fenn claimed that it was a matter of record that Bantam had been the first to suggest it. He argued that there was no more reason why Bantam could not build jeeps interchangeable with those constructed by Ford and Willys than there was in the case of the trucks being produced by White, Diamond T, and Auto-Car. Bantam stood ready to produce fifty to one hundred jeeps a day at any time General Somervell saw fit to put them into production. "I think you will agree with me," concluded the letter of Bantam's president, "that it has been quite a burden to stand by and see a quarter of a million of these cars purchased through negotiation, without once being given an opportunity to bid on them."[129]

At the verbal request of Douglas C. MacKeachie, a memorandum was prepared about this time for General Somervell, bearing the signature of Brigadier General J.L. Frink, the new Chief of the Motor Transport Division vice Lawes, once more setting forth the official stand of the QMC on Bantam's request for re-entry into the jeep programme. The memorandum enumerated several interrelated reasons why the OQMG felt that the placement of a jeep order with Bantam was "not warranted." Predominant among them was the fact that current production of Ford and Willys would soon reach a rate which would be more than sufficient to meet the Munitions Programme objective of 31 December 1942, including all defence aid requirements. Also, since Bantam did not contribute to the manufacture of component units of the jeep in their own factory, either tooling of additional sources for these components, especially the critical bottleneck items, would have to be provided or a portion of the production now flowing to Ford and Willys would have to be divided. Since the output of the Willys assembly line was now in balance with Spicer's production, and Ford's assembly line was in balance with the production of the critical jeep items produced within other Ford manufacturing units, the OQMG could see "no point gained in reducing the assembly schedule at Ford and Willys for the sole purpose of allowing assembly to be made by the American Bantam Car Company."

While the Quartermaster General's Office again expressed "sympathy with the position of the American Bantam Car Company in their desire for a place in the production picture," it felt that the facilities of Bantam could best be used for non-automotive production. It was "further believed that the great effort being exerted by the American Bantam Car Company to secure orders for production of ¼-ton trucks is motivated by a desire to create an advantageous position for the Company in the post-war automotive field."[130]

Oral conferences between Bantam's representatives and General Frink continued to be held during the last days of March. In addition to a long discussion with Mr. Fenn, General Frink wrote Somervell that he had also talked the matter over with another Bantam representative.[131] Presumably this was Richard B. Ransom, Consulting Engineer and Management Representative for Bantam, who wrote Douglas MacKeachie of this meeting, saying that on 27 March, General Frink had promised Mr. Fenn and himself a definite answer to Bantam's request for an immediate order for 6,000 jeeps, to be produced at a rate of 50 to 60 per day "to be continued to 1 July 1944, against the prospective Army requirements for the next two years." According to Ransom, this proposal had been suggested to him by General Frink as a possible solution advantageous to all concerned, and one which "would correct the injustice under which the Bantam Company now suffers."[132]

From these negotiations the Willys Company evidently gained the impression that Bantam had won its fight to manufacture jeeps, for on 29 March J.W. Frazer, Willys president, telegraphed a strong protest to the Under Secretary of War, Robert P. Patterson. According to the telegram, Willys' information had come straight from the horse's mouth—the Bantam Company. Referring to Willys' agreement with the Quartermaster Corps to turn over to any other source all patents, drawings, and engineering data necessary to the duplication of the Willys design, Frazer wired that "it was understood clearly at that time that we would have one-half of all the business the Government placed for this vehicle up to our capacity to produce as long as we gave satisfaction." Consideration of an additional third source for the jeep would be a violation of this agreement since Willys, with a capacity of 750 jeeps a day, was now only producing 394 daily in accordance with its contract. It would be both unfair to Willys and uneconomical to the Government to divide the jeep business further. The Willys jeep had thus far proven eminently satisfactory to the Armed Forces, the telegram said, and "we feel that repeat orders should come to us who have mastered the art of producing this vehicle in all its details and have kept abreast of Army developments and requirements."[133]

At the request of General Somervell in a memorandum to General Frink, a suggested reply to the Bantam letter of 23 March was prepared for General Somervell's signature. Similarly, a reply from the Under Secretary of War to Willys was also drafted by General Frink or his staff. Somervell's letter informed Bantam that to put it into production on the jeep would divert critical components from existing sources already under strain and would also involve unnecessary and unjustifiable duplication of tooling. It was General Somervell's understanding, however, that the Motor Transport Division was co-operating with Bantam "in an effort to place with you awards of other requirements which would not involve the duplication of facilities . . ."[134] Under Secretary Patterson's answer to Willys stated that investigation disclosed no official assurance whatever had been given Bantam that it was to receive an order for ¼-tons. Frazer was told that officers of the Bantam firm would confirm this. Investigation of Frazer's statement as to the purported agreement between Willys and the Quartermaster Corps for one-half of all the jeep business, revealed "no record of any such commitment to your company."[135] The "awards of other requirements" alluded to in General Somervell's letter of final rejection to Bantam on its request to be permitted to make jeeps again, was a letter of intent issued on the first of April to Bantam calling for 1,484 1-ton two-wheel trailers to be built and delivered by 30 September 1942, at a price to be negotiated later on,[136] but which General Frink estimated might be around $250 each.[137]

About this time another programme was under development for the building of two-wheel ¼-ton, cargo trailers that could be towed by the jeep, and Bantam was to share in the contracts for these as well. Development of this project had been recommended by the Infantry to provide more cargo space to aid the requirements of the transportation platoon. Approved by the Adjutant General, the development was now being conducted under the jurisdiction of the Quartermaster Corps. Twelve pilot models, incorporating standard units of the jeep wherever possible, had been ordered from Willys, to be distributed for service test to the Infantry, Air Corps, Engineers (later to be sent to the Medical Board), Signal Corps, Holabird Motor Base, and the Quartermaster Desert Test Command at Camp Seely, California. By May 1942 these units were in process of delivery, and the Motor Transport Subcommittee was recommending the ¼-ton trailer for standardisation.[138]

On 29 April letter contracts for 15,000 of the ¼-ton trailers were issued, 10,000 being awarded to Willys and 5,000 to Bantam. Both contractors estimated they could begin delivery the week of 15 July, seventy-five days being required for the tooling process. Willys expected eventually to reach a maximum of 200 per day, while Bantam was to start at a 600 per week rate. Both manufacturers were impressed with the necessity of as rapid production as possible, and every effort was to be made to better their schedules.[139]

Thus, while the Bantam Company, in contrast to the successful efforts of Ford, failed entirely to regain for itself a place in the jeep programme—a position that seemingly would have been of inestimable publicity value to it in any postwar competition with Willys and Ford on rival commercial versions or adaptations of the jeep—it did finally emerge from its turbulent, two-year fight for contracts against far weightier opponents, with some consolation in the form of these ¼-ton trailer awards. Bantam probably had thought,

when it built the first jeep models back in 1940 and watched them become a sensational success, that it had hit the "jackpot" and would not only benefit immediately from steady Army contracts but would also be in a favourable position to break into the low-priced commercial field after the war against the domination of the Big Three—General Motors, Ford, Chrysler—as well as against such remaining independents as Willys, Studebaker, and Hudson. It remains to be seen whether it will be able to combat successfully in the postwar period the advertising claims Willys is certain to make to having designed the standardised ¼-ton for the Army, as well as any Ford might make to having produced great quantities of them, with its own claim of having been the originator of the jeep.[140]

NOTES to CHAPTER II

1   *Truman Committee Hearings*, Testimony of Francis H. Fenn, 6 August 1941; see also *Standard Corporation Records*, June 1943.

2   *Standard Corporation Records*, June 1943.

3   In August 1938, the RFC loaned the American Bantam Company $275,000, of which a local bank took $50,000. In August 1941, the unpaid balance on this loan was $256,960. The loan was secured by a lien on the plant and equipment appraised at $862,000. The following June a second loan for $100,000 was authorised, the unpaid balance of which in 1941 was $7,352. In August 1940, Bantam borrowed $125,000, plus an additional $10,000 in November, to finance the building of the first seventy jeeps. These loans were subsequently paid in full. In December 1940, $1,300,000 was authorised by the RFC to enable the company to make 1,500 jeeps. Upon the completion of the contract this loan also was liquidated. Finally, in June 1941, a further loan of $1,094,870 was made for an additional thousand jeeps.

   Willys-Overland borrowed $2,500,000 from the RFC in June 1939. As in the Bantam transaction, a lien on the plant and equipment appraised at $7,400,000 secured the loan. Under the agreed amortisation payments, this loan by August 1941 was reduced to a balance of $2,088,658. A second loan of $1,290,000 was made to Willys in February 1941, to finance the manufacture of 1,500 jeeps. Security on this loan was through an assignment of the contract with the War Department, the value of which was approximately $1,400,000. Letters of Jesse H. Jones, Federal Loan Administrator, to John D. Biggers, Director, Division of Production, OPM, 9 August 1941 in *Truman Committee Hearings*, Exhibits 99 and 100, Appendex, page 2268.

4   QM 451 M-P (Proc. 398-41-9) (Trucks, ¼-ton 4x4), 2nd endorsement, OQMG to AG, 1 November 1940.

5   "Proceedings of Motor Transport Subcommittee, QMC Technical Committee" 18 October 1940.

6   *Ibid.*

7   QM 451 (Proc. 398-41-9), Charles H. Payne, Asst. to President, American Bantam Car Company, to the Hon. Henry L. Stimson, Secretary of War, 14 October 1940.

8   "Proceedings of Motor Transport Sub-Committee, QMC Technical Committee", 18 October 1940.

9   *Ibid*, Infantry Nonconcurrence, 21 October 1940.

10 *Ibid*, Field Artillery Nonconcurrence, 21 October 1940.

11 *Ibid*, Special Concurrence of the Cavalry, 21 October 1940.

12 QM 451 (M-P) (398-41-9), QMG to AG, "Procurement of Fifteen Hundred (1,500) Trucks. ¼-ton (4x4)," 22 October 1940.

13 *Ibid*, Eugene M. Rice, Willys-Overland, to Lt. Col. J. Van Ness Ingram, QMC, 18 October 1940.

14 *Ibid*, AG to QMG, "Procurement of Fifteen Hundred (1,500) Trucks, ¼-ton 4x4, 1st endorsement, 29 October 1940.

15 QM 451 (Proc. 398-41-9), AG 451 (10-22-40) M-D, AG to QMG, 3rd endorsement, 5 November 1940.

16   QM 451 (M-P) (Proc. 398-41-9), QMG to General R.C. Moore, 6 November 1940.

17   The Advisory Commission to the Council of National Defense was the predecessor of the OPM and NPB. Its approval, through clearance with Commissioner William S. Knudsen, had to be obtained for all War Department contracts amounting to $500,000 or more. OASW to QMG, "Approval of important purchases by Advisory Commission to the Council of National Defense," 10 June 1940; *ibid*, 13 June 1940. For a complete description of the functions of this Commission in relation to QMC procurement, see H.B. Yoshpe, "Streamlining Procurement Methods in the Quartermaster Corps," Historical Section, OQMG.

18   The first shipment of jeeps by Bantam on the 1,500 order, 31 March 1941, was 52, and a peak of 65 to 68 per day was reached later on. This was for one eight-hour shift and represented, according to the president of the Bantam Company, only 60% of the total productive capacity of its assembly line. For three eight-hour shifts per day, it was claimed that 275 to 300 jeeps could be produced daily, without further tooling. *Truman Committee Hearings*, Testimony of Francis H. Fenn and Lt. Col. Edwin S. Van Deusen, 6 August 1941.

19   This statement was typical of the difference in viewpoint between the using arms and the procuring service on the purchase of motor vehicles. In the case of the jeep, the Infantry and the other using arms apparently felt that since they had to live and fight with this equipment they should have a voice in the development and procurement decisions. The QMC attitude above was again expressed in somewhat different words by Colonel Van Deusen at the congressional investigation the following year when he said, "The Infantry is not a procuring agency, and we do not feel that the Infantry, not being a procuring agency, is qualified to judge all those phases of procurement . . . They use them. They don't buy them and they don't have to maintain them." *Truman Committee Hearings*, Testimony of Lt. Col. Edwin S. Van Deusen, QMC, 6 August 1941.

20   General Barzynski was head of the Motor Transport Division from 26 July 1940, at the time it was given separate divisional status within the QMC, to September 1941, when he was granted leave of absence. Colonel Herbert J. Lawes (Commanding Officer at Holabird) was designated Acting Chief, effective 11 September 1941. On 19 January 1942, Brigadier General James L. Frink was appointed Chief of MT, effective the following day, and remained in charge of the division until its transfer to Ordnance the following August. OQMG Office Order No. 52, 30 July 1940; *ibid*, No. 197, 9 September 1941, ibid, No. 14, 19 January 1942.

21   QM 451 (Proc. 398-41-9), Charles H. Payne, Asst. to the President, American Bantam Company, to Brigadier General Joseph E. Barzynski, QMC, 11 November 1940.

22   *Truman Committee. Hearings*, Testimony of Mr. John D. Biggers, 13 August 1941.

23   *Ibid.*

24   Of this policy, Colonel Douglas Dow, QMC Motor Transport Division, had this to say: "Policy was definitely see-sawing as of this date between the advantages of complete standardisation obtainable then only by buying from a single manufacturer as against dual sources which would ensure delivery in the event of various contingencies and also give us a competitive element to keep prices in line . . ." Statement by Colonel Dow, MT Historical Files, Historical Section, OQMG.

25   *Truman Committee Hearings*, Testimony of Mr. John D. Biggers, 13 August 1941.

26   QM 451 (Proc. 398-41-9), John D. Biggers to QMG, 14 November 1940.

27 In accordance with the directive from the Adjutant General, 5 November, the OQMG had entered into negotiation with the American Bantam Company. On the basis of 1,500 trucks Bantam had reduced its price offer from the $1,123 per unit quotation set for the 500, to $955.59 less one per cent for cash in ten days. The total net contract consideration was $1,419,051.15. Deliveries were to be 50 units for the week of 10 March 1941, 100 units for the week of 17 March, and the balance, at the rate of fifty truck per working day by 30 April. QM 451 (Proc. 398-41-9), F.H. Fenn, American Bantam, to Lt. Col. J. Van Ness Ingram, Purchasing and Contracting Officer, Holabird, 6, 7, 8 November 1940; *ibid*, QMG to Commissioner William S. Knudsen, 7 November 1941; *ibid*, QMC to ASW, 8 November 1940.

28 *Ibid*, Ford Motor Company to QMG, 9 November 1940.

29 *Ibid*, QMG to ASW, 19 November 1940.

30 QM 161 (Ford Motor Co.) (398-qm-8887), Lt. Col. Douglas Dow (for the QMG) to ASW, 20 December 1940.

31 *Ibid*, 3rd endorsement, Brigadier General J.E. Barzynski to Holabird, 27 December 1940.

32 I.F. Stone, "Behind the Ford Contract," *PM*, New York, 14 December 1940.

33 I.F. Stone, "Ford Still Gets the Breaks Even if it Does Jam Defense" *The Nation* 30 December 1940; See also *PM*, 30 December 1940.

34 The "Ford" in this concern was not Henry Ford.

35 United Press, "Thomas Protests Contracts To Ford," *The Nation*, 30 December 1940.

36 QM 451 (Proc. 398-41-9), Lt. Col. E.S. Van Deusen to John D. Biggers, "Comments on Article Regarding Ford in 30 December 1941, *PM*, 6 January 1941.

37 I.F. Stone, "Army Alters 'Midget' Car to Please Henry Ford," *PM*, 19 January 1941.

38 For the report of the House Committee on Military Affairs, on the jeep, issued 23 June 1942, see *infra*, Chapter II.

39 I.F. Stone, "Ford Contract Inquiry Urged", *PM*, 24 January 1941.

40 QM 451 (Proc. 398-41-9), Willys-Overland to Lt. Col. J. Van Ness Ingram, Holabird, 27 November 1940.

41 QM 161 (Ford Motor Company), (398-qm-8887), Lt. Col. Douglas Dow to ASW, 20 December 1940.

42 QM 451 (Proc. 398-41-9), Willys-Overland to Lt. Col. J. Van Ness Ingram, Holabird, 27 November 1940.

43 *Ibid*, Memorandum of verbal approval from Lt. Col. H.S. Aurand, G-4, to Lt. Col. Douglas Dow, 3 December 1940.

44 *Ibid*, QMG to ASW, "Negotiation for Motor Vehicle Equipment," 5 December 1940.

45 QM 161, Willys-Overland Motors, Inc. "Report of Pilot Model Vehicle, ¼-ton, 4x4, Command Reconnaissance truck, Contract No. W-398-qm-8888", 8 January 1941.

46 *Ibid.* Mechanical failures such as these were the rule, rather than the exception, for all pilot models subjected to the severe Holabird test. In the case of the jeep, the Bantam and Ford models were given equally rigorous tests. Breakdown of pilot models was purposely attempted in order to reveal faults in design, structure, and materials, which would have to be corrected before the vehicle was accepted. In this connection, Colonel Van Deusen told the Truman Committee: "I don't recall a single new production vehicle pilot model that has passed through those engineering tests that has not required some minor changes and in some cases, comparatively major changes, in order to make the vehicle . . . acceptable under the award." *Truman Committee Hearings*, Testimony of Lt. Col. Edwin S. Van Deusen, 6 August 1941. See also fn. 38, p. 32-33. For comparative field tests of all three jeep models, see *infra*, Chapter II.

47 *Ibid.*

48 Minutes of Quartermaster Corps Technical Committee", 22 January 1941.

49 QM 451 (Military Characteristics), Major General R.C. Moore, Deputy Chief of Staff to QMG, "Contract for manufacture of light cars," 8 February 1941.

50 *Ibid*, 1st Memorandum Endorsement, QMG to Deputy Chief of Staff, 5 March 1941.

51 QM 161, Willys-Overland Motors, Inc., Contract No. W-398-qm-8888, Major R.G. Amlong, Asst. Purchasing and Contracting Officer to Willys, 8 February 1941; *ibid*, Lt. Col. J. Van Ness Ingram, Purchasing and Contracting Officer, to Willys, 11 February 1941.

52 QM 451 (Proc. 398-41-9), I.F. Stone, "Willys-Overland Gets Army Favor on Midget Cars", *PM*, 16 February 1941.

53 MCM No. 8a, 27 June 1941; USA-LP-91-997A, 7 July 1941.

54 QM 400.112 (Truck, 1/4-ton, 4x4), Sub-Committee on Motor Transportation to QMC Technical Committee, "Revision of MCM No. 8a," 26 August 1941.

55 MCM No. 8d, 3 July 1942.

56 *Ibid.*

57 QM 161 (Ford Motor Company) (398-qm-8887), Lt. Col. Douglas Dow to ASW, 20 December 1940.

58 *Truman Committee Hearings*, Testimony of Lt. Col. E.S. Van Deusen, 6 August 1941.

59 *Ibid*, Testimony of F.H. Fenn, 6 August 1941.

60 QM 451 (Neg. Amer. Bantam Car Co.), W 398-qm-8886, Letters from American Bantam to Holabird, 26 March, 1 April 1941.

61 *Truman Committee Hearings*, Testimony of Lt. Col. E.S. Van Deusen, 6 August 1941.

62 QM 400.112 (Truck, 1/4-ton, 4x4), CI 451.4/9615, Chief of Infantry to President, Infantry Board, "Tests of 1/4-ton Trucks, Ford and Overland," 15 May 1941.

63 *Ibid*, Test Section, Infantry Board, Fort Benning, Georgia to President, Infantry Board, "Partial Report of Comparative Tests . . . Bantam, Ford, and Willys 1/4-ton, 4x4, Trucks," 22 July 1941.

64 *Ibid*, Infantry Board to Chief of Infantry, 31 July 1941.

65 *Ibid*, Chief of Infantry to QMG, 11 August 1941.

66 *Ibid*, QMG to Holabird, 15 August 1941; Colonel N.J. Lawes, Commanding Officer, Holabird, to QMG, 1st endorsement 26 August 1941.

67 *Ibid*, OQMG to AG, 3 September 1941.

68 *Truman Committee Hearings*, Testimony of F.H. Fenn, 6 August 1941.

69 QM 451 (Neg. Ford Motor Co.), Holabird to QMG, "Informal request for Quotation 'A1'" 8 May 1941; *ibid*, OQMG to Holabird, 1st endorsement 23 May 1941.

70 *Truman Committee Hearings*, Testimony of Lt. Col. E.S. Van Deusen, 6 August 1941.

71 *Ibid*, These memoranda were read to the Committee by Colonel Van Deusen.

72 See *supra*, fn.11, page 16, see also review of WD motor standardisation policy, *supra* pages 41-46.

73 *Truman Committee Hearings*, Testimony of John D. Biggers, 13 August 1941.

74 QM 451.2 (¼-ton, 4x4), QMC to General Moore, Deputy Chief of Staff, "Procurement of Trucks, ¼-ton, 4x4", 11 July 1941.

75 QM 451 M-P (Proc. 398-42-Neg.1), 16,000 Trucks, ¼-ton, 4x4, W-398-qm-10757, General Barzynski, WT Division, to QMG, 30 July 1941.

76 *Ibid*.

77 *Ibid*.

78 *Ibid*, "Approval of Negotiated Contract", 31 July 1941; "Request for Contract Clearance", 31 July 1941.

79 *Truman Committee Hearings,*Testimony of John D. Biggers, 13 August 1941.

80 QM 451 M-P (Proc. 398-42-Neg-1), 16,000 Trucks ¼-ton, 4x4, W-398-qm-10757, QMG to USW, 31 July 1941.

81 *Ibid*, Lt. Col. E.S. Van Deusen to Holabird, "Award . . . No. 398-42-Neg-1", 1 August 1941.

82 QM 161 Willys-Overland Motors, Inc., W-398-qm-10757, Assistant Purchasing and Contracting Officer to Procurement Control Branch, OQMG, 2 September 1941.

83 QM 095 M-P (Willys-Overland Inc.), Lt. Col. E.S. Van Deusen to Mr. Julius H. Amberg, "House Committee Investigation", 14 October 1941.

84 Senate Resolution 71, 77th Cong., 1st Sess., 1 March 1941.

85 Harry B. Yoshpe, *The Small Business Man and Quartermaster Contracts, 1940-1942*, Historical Section, OQMG. This study covers the general history of QMC procurement and contract policies in relation to the problem of contract distribution.

86 See *supra* Chapter I. In December 1941, it was decided in the QMC that in respect to the distribution of standardised motor equipment contracts, "the principle of standardisation, as established by the QMC and approved by the OUSW would take precedent over the policy of contract distribution." OQMG Daily Activity Report, Vol. 6, No. 5, 5 December 1941. Later next year, General Frink, Director of Motor Transport, wrote: "Standardisation and the policy of multiple suppliers is naturally in conflict." QM 451 M-P, Director, MT, to OQMG Director of Procurement, Legal Division, "Adequacy of Production Sources," 22 April 1942.

87 *Truman Committee Hearings,* Testimony of Francis H. Fenn, 6 August 1941. Bantam was not alone in regarding the changes in the specifications under which the bids for the 16,000 jeeps were based as favouring Ford. Willys also charged this in a memorandum to the Secretary of War's Office. However, Messrs. Canady and Frazier, the company's top officials, later apologised for several statements which seemed to imply that such specifications had been designed intentionally to eliminate Willys, stating that the paper had been prepared by a subordinate and that they did not wish to make such an implication. QM 095 (Willys-Overland Motors Inc.), Julius H. Amberg, Special Assistant to the Secretary of War to QMG, "Reconnaissance Cars," 17 July 1941.

88 *Truman Committee Hearings,* Testimony of Lt. Col. Edwin S. Van Deusen, QMC, 6 August 1941.

89 *Ibid,* Testimony of John D. Biggers, 13 August 1941.

90 See *supra*, Chapter II.

91 This general motor procurement policy was to govern procurements during the balance of FY 1941 and FY 1942. As proposed by the OQMG in a letter to the USW, 15 April 1941, and approved by that official 24 April 1941, it read: "Vehicle types and models now in service and being currently procured to be duplicated . . . to the maximum production capacity of the manufacturing organisations which have delivered satisfactory equipment during FY 1941. Requirements beyond the capability of current or recent contractors to duplicate items to be met by procurement from manufacturers who have submitted satisfactory pilot or test model vehicles." QM 451 M-P, QMC MT Division, Procurement Branch, to QMC, Procurement & Control Division, Procurement Control Branch, "Distribution of Defense Orders," 29 September 1941.

It should be noted that the above general policy differed materially from the specific procurement policy for the jeep advocated by the QMC in 1940 at which time it had favoured the inclusion of the additional sources of Ford and Willys for purposes of further development. It should also be noted that no attempt was made to apply this general policy to the purchase of the 16,000 jeeps in July 1941, since that would have meant the retention of Bantam and Willys as producers of the jeep as well; this would have resulted in the loss of standardisation because of the differences in design between the three jeep models. Since the QMC argued that there was not time to design a standard jeep which could be produced by all three manufacturers, the only way it could acquire the vast production resources of Ford for the manufacture of the jeep, without loss of standardisation, would be through Ford becoming the sole supplier of this vehicle.

92 QM 161, Julius H. Amberg to Colonels Van Deusen and Dow, "House Committee Investigation," 10 October 1941.

93 QM 095 M-P (Willys-Overland Inc.), Lt. Col. E.S. Van Deusen to Julius H. Amberg "House Committee Investigation", 14 October 1941. The general epidemic of strikes in the automobile industry at about this time had a serious effect on the production of Willys and its subcontractors and also affected the Ford and Bantam orders for 1,000 jeeps each. Labour disputes of one form or another continued to hamper Willys deliveries well into 1942. Among the plants affected from time to time were the H.A. Douglas Mfg. Co., Bronson, Michigan, making blackout switches, socket assemblies, etc., 23 September 1941; the Midland Steel Products Co., Cleveland, Ohio, makers of jeep frames, 29 September 1941; the Mather Spring Company, Toledo, Ohio, 8 October 1941; Spicer, Toledo, Ohio, 10 October 1941; Republic Steel, 31 January 1942; Detroit Nut Company, 16 February 1942; Great Lakes Steel Corp., Ecorse, Michigan, 3 March 1942. While all of these strikes generally were settled in short order, their cumulative effect could not fail to be serious. At the Willys plant itself, a strike was threatened as early as 8 September 1941, but by 21 October, difficulties had been settled. On 1 June 1942, a slow-down began at the Willys plant which the company reported to have increased considerably by 10 June. OQMG Daily Activity Reports, September 1941-March 1942; OQMG Weekly Progress Report, 2-8 June 1942; QM 161, Willys-Overland Motors, Inc., W-398-qm-10757, September 1941-February 1942.

94 *Investigation of the National Defense Program, Interim General Report of the House Military Affairs Committee, 23 June 1942.* pages 285-287. By 15 November 1941, Willys was delinquent on its deliveries of jeeps. Whereas 370 jeeps should have been delivered by 8 November, actually no deliveries were made. Recognising the difficulties encountered because of the strike conditions, Motor Transport requested Willys to submit a revised schedule. The new Willys schedule proposed delivery at the rate of 394 jeeps per day. QM 161 M-P (Willys-Overland Motors, Inc. Contract W-398-qm-10757), Lt. Col. J. Van Ness Ingram to Willys, 15 November 1941; QM 451 (Proc. 398-42-Neg. 1), 16,000 Trucks ¼-ton, 4x4-w-398-qm-10757, Major Robinson to Lt. Lovell and Colonel Dow, 23 December 1941.

95 QM 451 (Proc. 398-42-Neg-1) 16,000 Trucks, ¼-ton, 4x4, W-398-qm-10757, Ford Motor Company to OQMG Motor Transport Division, 6 August 1941.

96 *Ibid*, Lt. Col. Ingram to Colonel Van Deusen, 8 August 1941.

97   *Ibid*, Chief, Contract Control Branch to Chief, Procurement Branch, 13 August 1941.

98   *Ibid*, Chief, Motor Transport Division, to Chief, Procurement Branch, WT Division, 22 August 1941.

99   QM 161, Willys-Overland Motors, Inc, Wardon Canady, Chairman of Board, to Contracting Officer, Holabird, 10, 13 October 1941.

100   QM 161 PC-Proc. (Ford Motor Company), QMC to USW, 14 October 1941.

101   *Ibid*, 1st endorsement, 14 October 1941. Actually this letter of intent had been prepared on 4 October and had been signed by the Ford Company as of that date. QM 161 Ford Motor Co. 398-qm-10977, Ford Motor Company to OQMG, 19 November 1941.

102   QM 451 M-P (Neg-Ford Motor Co.), QMG to OPM Director of Purchases, 15 October 1941, with approval stamped 16 October. Signing for Douglas C. MacKeachie, Director of Purchases, was his assistant, Hiram S. Brown. Signing for the Quartermaster Corps, was Colonel H.J. Lawes, who by this time was acting Chief of Motor Transport, having replaced General Barzynski, 11 September. See Note 71.

103   QM 095 (Willys-Overland Motors, Inc), Lt. Col. E.S. Van Deusen to Mr. John W. Snyder, 15 October 1941.

104   OQMG Daily Activity Report, Vol. 4, No. 14, 16 October 1941.

105   Office of Govt. Reports, "This Week in Defense", 24 October 1941.

106   QM 095 M-P Lt. Col. J. Van Ness Ingram to Ford Motor Company, Alexandria, Virginia, 21 October 1941.

107   QM 451 (Neg-Willys-Overland Motors, Inc.), Lt. Col. J. Van Ness Ingram to Willys-Overland, 10 November 1941.

108   QM 451 M-P (Neg-Ford Motor Co.), W-398-qm-10977, Col. H.J. Lawes to the USW, "Approval of Negotiated Contract" 9 January 1942; PC-E 161 (Negotiated Contract) (Ford Motor Company), 1st endorsement, 10 January 1942.

109   *Ibid*.

110   Now that competition had been eliminated and the negotiated form of contract was being employed, the price of the jeep made by Willys also advanced. From its low bid of $748.74 per unit, which took the contract for the 16,000 jeeps from Ford by underbidding that concern by $34 per jeep, a subsequent contract with Willys for 43,601 jeeps was negotiated at a net unit cost of $829.70 less ½% for payment within 10 days, equalling a net price of $825.55. Change orders on both Ford and Willys at times caused even further fluctuations. In January 1942, the cost of the jeep was said to be approximately $875. In April 1942, it was being quoted at approximately $855. QM 451 (Neg. Willys-Overland Motors, Inc.), 43,061 Trucks (¼-ton, 4x4) W-398-qm-11423, Letter of Intent, Lt. Col. Ingram to Willys, 29 December 1941; *ibid*, OQMG to Holabird, "Negotiated Contract W-398-qm-11423 with Willys-Overland Motors Inc." 17 May 1942; memorandum from Motor Transport to OQMG General Service Division, "Information for Radio Program," 19 January 1942; QM 451 M-E (Ordnance), OQMG to Chief of Ordnance, "Patrol Cars", 28 April 1942.

111   QM 451, Ford Motor Company to Lt. Col. J. Van Ness Ingram, "Re: Contract No. W-398-qm-10977", 18 February 1942; *ibid*, Ingram to Holabird, "Change Order to Contract W-398-qm-10977", 24 February 1942.

112   *Ibid*, Lt. Col. Ingram to Holabird, 30 March 1942.

113   QM 451 (Neg. Ford Motor Co.), "Tools for Mfg. of ¼-Ton, 4x4 Tr.," Hiram S. Brown to QMG, 16 October 1941.

114   *Ibid*, Lt. Col. Ingram to Acting Chief, Motor Transport, 23 October 1941.

115   *Ibid*, Executive Assistant to Acting Chief, Motor Transport, 23 October 1941.

116   *Ibid*, Colonel Lawes to QMG, 23 October 1941.

117   *Ibid*, QMG to Col. Hiram S. Brown, OPM, 14 November 1941. The inclusion of a clause governing the ownership of machine tools by the Government was being applied to other contracts as well as the one to Ford. For example, the Procurement Control Branch of the OQMG Planning and Control Division notified Motor Transport that its letter of intent to the Fargo Motor Corporation (Chrysler), 10 November 1941, covering the proposed purchase of 5,100 ¾-ton, low-silhouette trucks had been approved by the Quartermaster General subject to the incorporation of a provision in the formal contract for Government ownership of all special tools, jigs and fixtures. QM Pc-Proc, Procurement Control Branch, P & C Division to Chief, Motor Transport Division, "Letter of Intent—Fargo Motor Corporation", 10 November 1941.

118   QM 461 (Neg. Ford Motor Company) (W-398-qm-11424), Lt. Col. Ingram to Ford Motor Company, 29 December 1941.

119   QM 451 (Neg. Willys-Overland Motors, Inc), W-398-qm-11423, Lt. Col. Ingram to Willys-Overland, 29 December 1941.

120   QM 461 (Neg. Ford Motor Company) (W-398-qm-11424), Major Ralph G. Boyd, QMC Contracting Officer, to Ford Motor Company, 22 April 1942.

121   QM 451 (Neg. Willys-Overland Motors, Inc), W-398-qm-11423, Major Boyd to Willys-Overland, 19 May 1942.

122   QM 451.2 (Trucks, ¼-ton, 4x4), Major Boyd to Deputy Director, QMC, Motor Transport Service, Procurement Division, Detroit, Michigan, 3 August 1942.

123   QM 095 M-C (American Bantam Car Co.), QMG to the Honourable Joseph S. Guffey, US Senate, 27 October 1941.

124   QM 095 G-C (American Bantam Car Co.), QMG to Senator Guffey, 19 November 1941.

125   "Survey of the Army Supply Program", QMC Motor Transport Service, 8 May 1942. Total estimated vehicle requirements for 1943 were 1,196,516 and for the first six months of 1944, 1,249,881, or a grand total for the two and a half years of 3,404,940 vehicles of all types.

126   *Ibid*. The breakdown figures for these 179,177 jeeps were: AT — 79,495; DA — 97,402 and other Arms and Services — 2,280.

127   *Ibid*. The exact figure was 31,227.

128   *Ibid*. Jeep procurement requirements for 1943 were estimated at 195,069, broken down into 92,667 for AT; 97,402 for DA; and 5,000 for other Arms and Services. For the first six months of 1944, estimated requirements were 194,555, with 143, 354 for AT; 48,701 for DA; and 2,500 for other Arms and Services.

129   Letter, Francis H. Fenn to General Brehon B. Somervell, 23 March 1942, copy on file in OQMG Historical Section.

130   QM 451 M-E (Trucks, ¼-ton, 4x4), Brig. Gen. J.L. Frink to General Brehon B. Somervell, "American Bantam Car Company", 24 March 1942.

131   QM 451.2 M-AL (Jeeps), Brig. Gen. Frink to General Somervell. "American Bantam Motor Car Company," 1 April 1942.

132   QM 095 (American Bantam Car Co.), Richard B. Ransom to Douglas MacKeachie, 4 April 1942. Had this deal gone through the jeeps would have been of the four-wheel steer type. See *infra*, Chapter II.

133   Telegram, J.W. Frazer to Under Secretary of War, Robert P. Patterson, 29 March 1942, copy on file in OQMG Historical Section.

134   Letter, General Brehon B. Somervell to F.H. Fenn (no date), copy on file in OQMG Historical Section.

135   Letter, Under Secretary of War, Robert P. Patterson, to J.W. Frazer, 1 April 1942, copy on file in OQMG Historical Section. According to General Frink in his letter of 1 April, to Generasl Somervell, Bantam denied ever having told Willys it was to receive an order.

    Frazer's contention that Willys was supposed to receive half of the jeep contracts placed, was probably based on both Willys' original agreement with Motor Transport to permit Ford to make jeeps of Willys design and the later Motor Transport policy of putting Ford and Willys on a "fifty-fifty" basis. See *supra* Chapter II.

136   QM 451 (American Bantam Car Co.) (W-398-qm-12837), Lt. Col. J. Van Ness Ingram to the American Bantam Car Co. 1 April 1942.

137   QM 451.2 M-AL (Jeeps), General Frink to General Somervell, 1 April 1942.

138   SPQME 451.3 (Trailer, ¼-ton, two-wheel, Cargo), QMC Motor Transport Subcommittee to QMC Technical Committee, 8 May 1942. The Cargo trailer for the jeep was standardised by the SOS, 20 June 1942, with the QMC being made responsible for its storage and issue. *Ibid*, SOS to QMG, 3rd endorsement, 20 June 1942.

139   *Ibid*, Brig. Gen. J.L. Frink to Commanding General, SOS, 16 May 1942.

140   An idea of what continuation in the jeep programme might have meant for Bantam may be garnered from a report of what the jeep business has helped to accomplish for Willys, which, although many times Bantam's size, was in an analogous position in 1940 insofar as straitened financial circumstances were concerned. In the Willys Company's annual report for the fiscal year ending with September 1943, W.M. Canaday, president, told stockholders that the net profit for the year amounted to $3,010,901, equivalent to $1.32 a share of common stock after preferred dividend requirements. This was after all charges had been provided for, including taxes of $20,015,000 and reserves of $4,408,771 for contingencies and reconversion to normal business. In noting that the concern's backlog of government contracts approximated $225,000,000, Canaday reported that the Willys military jeep had created a background of international good-will against which the company would build its future in the postwar world. *The New York Times*, 5 January 1944.

CHAPTER III

Two Adaptations of the Jeep: 4-Wheel Steer and Amphibious

Besides the story of the jeep proper recounted in the preceding chapters, two distinct variations or adaptations of the jeep chassis took place in connection with its development during the period 1940-1942: the four-wheel steer jeep and the amphibian jeep. The first differed from the regular jeep in that steering could be applied to all four wheels at once instead of to the front wheels alone, thus permitting almost right-angle turns and "about-faces" from a straight course that were little short of amazing.[1] Like the orthodox jeep, the four-wheel steer was strictly a land-going vehicle. The second departure, the amphibian jeep, was a radical embodiment of the jeep chassis within a motor boat hull, which, with the addition of boat propulsion machinery, permitted travel on both land and sea. The four-wheel steer jeep, for reasons which will become apparent, never did become standardised by the Army; procured only in limited experimental quantities, it eventually was dropped entirely from the motor programme. The amphibian jeep, on the other hand, was successfully developed and standardised, and was used with considerable effectiveness by the Allies in the subsequent Sicilian and Italian landing operations of 1943.

The Four-Wheel Steer Jeep

In much the same fashion as the conventional ¼-ton, the story of the four-wheel steer jeep, stemming as it did from the original lot of seventy procured from the American Bantam Company in July 1940, eight of which were specified to be of the four-wheel steer type, was highlighted by technical differences of opinions between the using arms—this time principally the Cavalry— and the Quartermaster Corps over the military value of the four-wheel steer as opposed to the maintenance and production complications resulting from the standardisation of another motor vehicle. The Cavalry, then in the process of mechanization, fought hard to retain the four-wheel steer jeep because its manoevrability made it suitable for mechanized cavalry operations and tactics. It was successfully opposed by the Quartermaster Corps, however, which, in addition to considering the four-wheel steer a dangerous vehicle to operate, won its points on the maintenance and production problems involved when the matter had to be presented to General Somervell's office for adjudication. As in the procurement of the orthodox jeep, the Bantam Company also was centrally involved in this controversy. In its last attempt to obtain jeep contracts at the time it made its plea to General Somervell in March 1942, the contract for the 6,000 jeeps Bantam was demanding was for vehicles of the four-wheel steer type. As it finally turned out, the Quartermaster Corps was the victor on all counts, just as it had been in the case of the regular jeep.

Shortly after the original eight Bantams with four-wheel steering had been sent to the field for service testing, the question of further development and procurement of this type began to be considered by the Motor Transport subcommittee and the QMC Technical Committee. At the meeting of the subcommittee, 5 March 1941, the QMC representative questioned the need of both the two-wheel steer and the four-wheel steer, citing the added maintenance and production difficulties that would ensue in the future from the standardisation and procurement of both types.[2] To this the Cavalry representative replied that the partial reports of the Bantam received from the field thus far "indicated no particular difficulty had been experienced with this type of vehicle either in their mechanical construction insofar as four-wheel steer mechanism was concerned or in their operation." He declared that the reports received by the Cavalry on the four-wheel steer Bantams were, in fact, so favourable, especially in respect to their extremely short turning radius of eleven feet as compared to the nineteen feet required for the two-wheel steer models, as to justify additional procurement for further tests. At this meeting the Cavalry carried the day, as it was to do at all succeeding committee meetings on this question, and the subcommittee voted to carry the motion that one hundred of the four-wheel jeeps be procured in accordance with the MCM No. 8, 14 February 1941.[3]

When the QMC Technical Committee met a few days later to consider the subcommittee's recommendation, Colonel Van Deusen said that personally he did not concur in the subcommittee report and thought the whole jeep procurement programme would be delayed if it was adopted because of the difficulty that would be experienced in connection with the axle bottleneck. Nevertheless, after considerable discussion, the Infantry member moved that the four-wheel steer project be approved for further experiment and development, but under conditions that would not interfere with the balance of the jeep programme. The motion was seconded and carried.[4]

Within the next month certain members of both houses of Congress began to evince interest in the fate of this unconventional Bantam jeep which so successfully emulated the grasshopper, or, as another writer put it, was "the closest thing on the ground to piloting an airplane."[5] Whether Bantam was behind these inquiries is not known. At any rate, the Quartermaster General replied to each inquiry with identical letters dated 8 April, outlining the action recommended by the QMC Technical Committee at their March meeting and stating that the matter was now up for consideration by the General Staff. Each legislator was informed that while it was "understood . . . reports from the field at first were quite enthusiastic . . . this attitude has been modified in recent weeks." The policy of the Quartermaster General's Office, the letters said further, was "to adhere to the safeguard of not adopting any item unless it has first successfully withstood the proper field tests."[6]

At the next meeting of the QMC Technical Committee, three days later, a directive from the Adjutant General was read approving the purchase of fifty four-wheel steer jeeps, instead of one hundred, and transferring funds for this development in a sum not to exceed $60,000. The directive further specified that the Technical Committee was to recommend the distribution of these jeeps for test to the different arms and services. This the Committee did, allotting 36 to the Cavalry, six to the Armored Force, three each to the Coast and Field Artillery and two to the Quartermaster Corps.[7]

After the usual clearances had been obtained, Holabird was directed to negotiate a contract with the American Bantam Company at its bid price of $1,150 per vehicle, the total net cost of the contract amounting to $56,925 after deduction of the 1%—10 days discount.[8] Shortly thereafter the Quartermaster General held a conversation with the Assistant Chief of Staff and the Deputy Chief, Generals Reybold and Moore, in which both authorised the purchase of an identical number of the four-wheel steer jeeps from the Ford Motor Company. The Quartermaster General then directed Motor Transport to make this procurement from Ford.[9] Ford's price was $1,145 per jeep less $50 within 30 days, or a total net cost of $54,750 for the fifty.[10]

On 30 January 1942, the Motor Transport subcommittee met and recommended that the four-wheel steer jeep be standardised and issued in addition to the regular model. This action was taken despite the fact that a roll-call of all members present disclosed that no one was in agreement with the Cavalry's original proposal that the four-wheel steer jeep should be adopted to replace the two-wheel steer entirely. The Armored Force, desiring to have both favoured only partial adoption, while the reports of the Field Artillery, Coast Artillery and the Holabird Quartermaster Depot read at the meeting, evinced little enthusiasm for the four-wheel steer. The reason for the solid line-up of the using arms against the Quartermaster Corps on the voting therefore lay in their unanimously expressed opinion "that if one Arm or Service deemed the use of a certain vehicle essential to the accomplishment of its respective mission, that the other Arms or Services should not deny it that vehicle."[11] This solidarity against the Quartermaster Corps was illustrative of the solicitude with which the using arms guarded their prerogative of determining for themselves the military characteristics and military value of their own equipment.

Dissenting from this viewpoint, the Quartermaster Corps attached an official non-concurrence to the committee's recommendation, listing four objections to the proposal. The four-wheel steer jeep was seen as requiring twice as many of the steering drive end joints, the manufacture of which already was a production bottleneck; standardisation would prevent the free interchange of vehicles between the Cavalry and other arms and services; the maintenance problem would be further complicated by the additional stockage of required parts as well as by the extra work involved in the maintenance of the greater number of moving units; and finally it was believed that the employment of four-wheel steer jeeps would increase the accident rate.[12]

The above arguments were again presented by the Quartermaster Corps when the entire matter was thrashed out the following month before the QMC Technical Committee. Against these was the main contention of the Cavalry that all of its testing agencies had overwhelmingly recommended that the four-wheel steer be adopted 100% for that arm. "The objection of the Quartermaster Corps to safety is non-existent," declared the Cavalry representative, "and, in fact, some . . . tests have proved the four-wheel steer is not as dangerous as the two-wheel." According to him, the other reasons advanced by the QMC were not entirely justified either except from a production standpoint, since it forced a combat branch to use equipment it considered unsatisfactory. Backing up the Cavalry, the Armored Force representative stated that they wanted the four-wheel steer for their reconnaissance units. As for the spare parts problem, he saw little difference between the two jeep axles insofar as the stockage of parts was concerned.

Representatives of the other Army branches, although they themselves were not interested in the four-wheel steer for their own organizations, also backed the Cavalry's stand. The Infantry member said that he could testify from his own personal driving experience with the four-wheel steer jeep that there was no extra hazard to the driver. He also felt that the production problem was being "overstressed," since similar situations had existed in the past and had been overcome. The Field Artillery member stated that he wished to point out to the Quartermaster Corps "that more attention should be given to the mission for which the vehicle is intended instead of hindering the agency."

Seeing that the using arms were solidly arrayed against denying the Cavalry the vehicle it deemed desirable to effecting its mission, the Quartermaster representative suggested that the final decision be left to the General Staff. Whereupon a vote was taken with all in favour of adopting the four-wheel steer except the QMC Motor Division. The motion to adopt the recommendation of the subcommittee for standardisation and leave the final decision to the Commanding General of the Services of Supply, was then made, seconded, and carried.[13]

In the meantime, the Bantam Company evidently was pulling every string within its reach in its efforts to regain entry into the jeep programme. The letters of Fenn and Ransom to General Somervell and Douglas MacKeachie were both part of this drive. In addition to this letter to MacKeachie, Ransom apparently was also able to enlist the offices of Senator Robert R. Reynolds, Chairman of the Senate Military Affairs Committee, in calling MacKeachie's attention to the four-wheel steer jeep situation. On 9 March, Senator Reynolds wrote MacKeachie, recalling that when they had last talked over the jeep matter on 25 February, MacKeachie had indicated that Ransom should take up the question of the 6,000 four-wheel steer jeep order in person with the Quartermaster Corps. It was the Senator's recollection that should the Quartermaster refuse to give this order, or if there should be any delay in the proceedings, Ransom was to get in touch with either MacKeachie or Donald Nelson, who would act on the matter together or separately and "procure favourable action thereon."

This information had been conveyed by Senator Reynolds to Ransom who then called upon General Frink, Chief of the QMC Motor Transport Division. General Frink told Ransome "this order was dead," so far as the QMC knew. At the same time Frink informed Senator Reynolds that he did not wish to approve the order to Bantam until the standardisation question on the four-wheel steer had been settled.

In his letter Reynolds expressed puzzlement as to why the order for the 6,000 four-wheel steer jeeps to Bantam was being held up, especially since the vehicle had already been approved "four times" in committee meetings. Moreover, since January more than 100,000 of the regular two-wheel steer jeeps had been ordered from Willys and Ford, bringing the grand total of these two concerns to more than 287,500 jeeps. From all this, wrote the Senator, he could only "draw the deduction . . . that the Quartermaster Corps is so loaded up with these front steer car units as to prevent any trial of the four-wheel steer car units, and to prevent any orders from being given to the American Bantam Company." This, he added, was merely his deduction; if he were in error he wished to know it immediately.

"It strikes me that this four-wheel steer jeep is something that is needed by the Army, from all that I can gather . . . " Reynolds continued. "Why some several thousand . . . have not been ordered from the American Bantam Company is something that I am unable to understand . . . Mr. Ransome, it appears to me has been given the run-around. If his cars are not adaptable for Army use . . . if there is any reason why the Army doesn't want to make use of these four-wheel steer jeep types, he would like to know it."[14]

A copy of this letter was sent to General Frink by Reynolds and it was from this copy that the above has been quoted. No copy, or other information as to any reply MacKeachie may have made to Senator Reynolds was found in the OQMG records examined. The copy was signed and at the end there appeared in Reynolds' handwriting a postscript inquiring as to when Ransom might see General Frink.[15]

On 17 March, a memorandum from General Frink advised General Somervell's SOS headquarters of the QMC Technical Committee's action of 14 March.[16] Frink also addressed a similar communication to Douglas C. MacKeachie, in which he took issue with the Cavalry's statement that the four-wheel steer version of the jeep was highly desirable for Cavalry operations. The controlling factor in the adoption of such an item of equipment, General Frink thought, should be the inability of the using arm to carry out its mission successfully without the use of the item; it was the belief of his office "that the Cavalry cannot definitely state that their mission cannot be performed without the use of this type of vehicle." In conclusion, MacKeachie's attention was directed to the authority of the Commanding General of the SOS to either approve or disapprove the Technical Committee's recommendation.[17]

The decision of higher authority was received by the Quartermaster General one week later through a first endorsement from the SOS which stated:

> The undesirable features of increased maintenance, decreased interchangeability , and production difficulties inherent in the four-wheel steer, ¼-ton truck, are deemed to outweigh the performance advantages of this type. The adoption of the four-wheel steer ¼-ton truck is not favourably considered; no additional four-wheel steer trucks will be procured.[18]

This directive to discontinue the four-wheel steer jeep not only settled the issue within the Army, as between the Cavalry and the Quartermaster Corps, but it also determined once and for all that the American Bantam Company would make no further jeeps for the Army. As already noted, the letter of final rejection to Bantam's request for an order to manufacture 6,000 jeeps which was prepared for General Somervell's signature by Motor Transport was dated around 1 April—six days after the decision was made to abandon the four-wheel steer jeep entirely. Had Bantam's proposal been received favourably, the 6,000 ¼-tons called for by the proposed order undoubtedly would have been of the four-wheel steer type.

The Amphibian Jeep

It will be recalled that back in June 1940 when the Chief of Infantry first set up the requirement for a light vehicle with a minimum silhouette to replace the motorcycle for command and reconnaissance purposes, one of the conditions set forth was that, if feasible, the frame and body were to be designed so as to provide amphibious characteristics. If prevailing circumstances, such as a possible delay in the production of the test vehicles, did not permit the incorporation of the amphibious feature at the time, the Chief of Infantry desired that experimentation and development along this line be continued until successfully concluded. In view of the personnel-carrying and other uses to which the amphibian jeep was put three years later in landing operations by the Allies on Sicily and the Italian peninsula, this requirement may be regarded as an example of considerable foresight upon the part of the "Queen of Battles" branch of the Army.

Because of the complications attendant upon the development of the first seventy Bantam jeeps, as well as the further development and procurement difficulties connected with bringing Ford and Willys into the programme on the 4,500 jeep order, the amphibian jeep project did not get underway until March 1941. At that time the Quartermaster Corps Technical Committee met to consider the recommendation of the Motor Transport subcommittee to set up such a project in accordance withe the tentative military characteristics outlined by the Chief of Infantry the preceding January, which the subcommittee had now revised in two or three particulars. The original Infantry characteristics envisaged an amphibian vehicle that would have a maximum weight of 2,600 pounds and a maximum silhouette of forty inches; cross country ability and roadability equal to that of the regular ¼-ton jeep; capacity of three men and their equipment plus one light machine-gun with 2,000 rounds of .30 calibre ammunition; and all-wheel drive. Propulsion and steering in water was to be either by the wheels used on land or through a power take-off from the regular power train. The maximum speed in still water was to be five miles per hour, and the changeover from land to water operation was to be effected without any other appliances than those habitually carried on the vehicle, "with not to exceed one minute of delay incident to the changeover."

This time limit of "one minute" had been changed by the subcommittee to read "with the minimum possible delay." Likewise the maximum weight limit restriction had been removed and changed to "minimum practicable," and the maximum speed of five miles per hour in water had been revised to read "required speed in still water—about five miles per hour." With these few changes designed to facilitate development, the Technical Committee qpproved the subcommittee report.[19]

In the following month of April, the National Defence Research Committee was asked, through the War Department liaison unit, to co-operate by carrying on the necessary research work.[20] At the same time EDT Project No. 33-41 was set up at Holabird, 19 April, to study the general problem of converting different sizes of military vehicles to amphibians.[21] Beside the proposed jeep development there were then two other sizes under consideration, the Hofheins ½-ton and a projected 2½-ton amphibian, both of which should be mentioned here for purposes of rounding out the amphibian picture.

The Hofheins ½-ton (later in development, of ¾-ton capacity) was a product of the Amphibian Car Corporation, Buffalo, New York, and derived its name from the company's president, Roger W Hofheins. It had been submitted for Army consideration in the spring of 1941. Weighing approximately 5,500 pounds, it was capable of transporting seven men on land or water, and had additional cargo-carrying capacity when in water. It used the same engine and other regular components as in the ½-ton Dodge command cars and weapons carriers. The essential difference between the Hofheins and the contemplated jeep amphibian development was that the former was designed basically around the hull as the backbone of the vehicle, whereas the NDR Committee development was considering the addition of a hull to the standard jeep chassis.

Signal Corps Photo

Tentative military characteristics of the ½-ton amphibian as of 27 June 1941, required it to haul a payload of 1,000 pounds and have a gross weight of approximately 5,400 pounds. Speeds on land and in water were set at not less than 55 and 5 miles per hour, respectively. No provision was included in these characteristics for the mounting of armament, but by October, the .30 calibre machine gun or the aircraft type 37mm cannon was being considered. Six or seven of the Hofheins were contracted for under these military characteristics, and successful trials were held at Fort Belvoir, Virginia on 2 March 1942, a demonstration that was witnessed by the Motor Transport subcommittee.[22] However, after the successful development of the amphibious jeep built by Ford in 1942, little further was heard of the Hofheins amphibian.

Development of the 2½-ton amphibian took place almost concurrently with the jeep amphibian. Based upon the regular 2½-ton, 6x6, truck chassis built by General Motors' subsidiary, the Yellow Truck and Coach Manufacturing Company, the project was initiated in April 1941 by Colonel Van Deusen at the request of the Commanding General, Services of Supply. Both the NDR Committee and the Yellow Coach Company entered into an agreement to co-operate in the 2½-ton amphibian development. By May the tank tests were reaching their conclusion and the construction of full-scale pilot models was expected to be undertaken before the end of the month.[23]

The first pilot model of this GMC 2½-ton amphibian—dubbed the "duck" in conformance with the American propensity for attaching colourful, descriptive names to individual pieces of military equipment—was demonstrated before members of the Motor Transport subcommittee at the General Motors Proving Grounds, 12 June 1942. The design of the duck was deemed satisfactory, only minor construction changes being suggested by the subcommittee. Dimensions and performance figures of this large, powerful amphibian revealed that it had an overall length of 354 inches, width of 96 inches, and wheelbase of 164 inches. Without its rated 2½-ton load, it weighed seven tons and was capable of transporting approximately 35 men on land and 50 or more in water, depending on the freeboard required. The duck had a land speed of around 45 miles per hour and a speed of 6 miles per hour in water. On land it drove through all six wheels, just as in the regular 2½-ton, while in water the drive was through a rear-mounted propeller, the shaft of which, like the axles, pierced the hull through sealed tubes or openings. A cruising range of two hundred miles on land was attributed to the duck; in water this was cut down to fifty miles.[24]

In July 1942, the Quartermaster General was directed to issue a letter of intent initiating immediate procurement of 2,000 of these 2½-ton ducks from General Motors. It was desired that 600 be produced by 31 December and the balance by the following March.[25] Thus the duck, like the amphibian jeep, was ready for the invasions of Sicily and Italy in the summer and autumn of 1943, and proved to be a worthy partner to the smaller sea-going vehicle.

Returning to the development of the amphibious counterpart of the jeep itself, the project came close to being eliminated entirely in August 1941 when the Adjutant General requested its cancellation because of the then satisfactory situation in respect to the Hofheins ½-ton amphibian. But the Quartermaster Corps asked for re-consideration of the cancellation and this was granted.[26] This, perhaps, was a fortunate decision, for after Pearl Harbour put America into the war directly and President Roosevelt and Prime Minister Churchill later made the decision to send an American Expeditionary Force to North Africa, an intensive effort was made in the spring and summer of 1942 to put the amphibian jeep into immediate production. Judging from the extreme urgency with which this was attempted, it is a fair assumption that the amphibians were wanted for the African landings. However, the amphibian jeeps missed participating in these operations by a month or so because of various production and other complications. It hardly seems likely that it was intended to use the amphibian jeeps in the Guadalcanal operations which took place in August 1942, some time before the African landings in November. Even as early as May it was not expected that the amphibian jeep could be put into production before August.

The first hand-built model of the amphibian jeep was presented to the Army by the National Defense Research Committee in 18 February, 1942.[27] Two models were built, one by Ford and one by Marmon-

94

Herrington, but it was then decided to concentrate on Ford models exclusively, because of Ford's greater production capacity. The Ford model weighed 3,400 pounds, an increase of 1,000 pounds over the standard land jeep. Its length, width and wheelbase, measured in inches, were respectively, 187.6, 64 and 84. On land it was practically as fast as the regular jeep, having an approximate maximum speed of 60 miles per hour. In water its speed was about 7 miles per hour. The angle of approach was 37 degrees.[28]

A second model by Ford, known as Amphibian No. 3, followed hard on the heels of the first. In Amphibian No. 3, which was expected to be the production model, a few construction changes were made. In order to give increased capacity for both personnel and equipment, the seating arrangement was made similar to that of the standard jeep. The weight was reduced approximately 300 pounds and the angle of approach increased about 3 degrees. Improved speed and backing ability in water was obtained by moving the propeller forward and down. Hatches and cooling vents were rearranged for greater cooling efficiency, and the radiator decreased in size so that it was only slightly larger than the standard ¼-ton radiator.[29]

By May, Ford models Nos. 1 and 2 were at Holabird undergoing breakdown tests. The Marmon-Herrington model No. 1 was at Fort Belvoir, Virginia, where it was being observed by the Engineering Board. Ford model No. 3 had left the factory and was on its way to Fort Knox, Kentucky, where it was to be tested for three days. It was then scheduled to go for further trials to Fort Benning, Georgia, Fort Bragg, North Carolina, the Marine Base at Quantico, Virginia, and the QMC Holabird Depot, in that order; it was to arrive at the last destination about 26 May.[30]

In the meantime, on 10 or 11 April, Ford had been directed by General Frink to proceed at once with plans for the production of at least 5,000 amphibian jeeps.[31] At this time, the calculations of the Ground Forces indicated a total requirement of approximately 3,100 amphibian jeeps, but on this basis, General Somervell had increased the total to 5,000, which was thought to be the maximum amount that would be needed for 1942.[32] A letter contract was issued immediately, 11 or 12 April, confirming the telephonic authorisation of production to Ford and emphasizing that this production must be expedited.[33]

One week later the Motor Transport subcommittee met and acted to recommend the amphibian jeep for standardisation. Attached to the subcommittee's recommendation was a breakdown of the contemplated basis of issue, showing 1,400 for the Infantry, 574 for the Tank Destroyer, 549 for the Cavalry, 1,440 for the Armored Force, and 1,100 for the Signal Corps,[34] the total of which more than took care of the initial procurement of 5,000.

From this point on it was a race against time to get the amphibian jeeps rolling off the Ford assembly line and into the hands of the Army. Speed and more speed in production seemed to be the order of the day, from Generals Marshall and Somervell on down. While, naturally, none of the Quartermaster records of this period specifically indicated the Theatre of Operations for which these amphibian jeeps were intended, or the purpose for which they were to be used, it was fairly clear from the urgency expressed in the documents that large scale amphibious operations were not far off.

At a Motor Transport Policy Committee[35] meeting held 8 May, between General Frink and his chief executives, including Colonels Campbell, Howard, Ingram, Van Deusen, Wilson, Richmond, Tupper and Moran, General Frink stressed to Colonel Ingram the extreme importance of expediting delivery of the first 5,000 amphibian jeeps. With specifications now complete, it was brought out at the meeting that Ford had been instructed to tool up for fifty per day. General Frink ordered this doubled to one hundred per day. When Colonel Van Deusen revealed that production was not to start until August, General Frink remarked that this would be too late, for the first 5,000 were needed in September. He impressed upon everyone the importance of giving the amphibian jeep the highest possible priority, stating that General Marshall himself was personally interested in the matter.[36] The following day General Frink's instructions were carried out, and Ford was directed by Colonel Ingram to tool up for production at the rate of 3,000 amphibian jeeps per month. "The need for them is very urgent," wrote Ingram, "and it is requested that you take every step possible to expedite the production. . ."[37]

Clearance for machinery and equipment to be used in the production of the ¼-ton amphibians was obtained from the WPB, 23 May, after some difficulties with its Plant Site Board. The Board had originally ruled that the amphibian jeeps would have to be assembled at some outside Ford plant because of the critical labour supply situation in Detroit. Reconsideration of the decision was requested by General Frink on 22 May in a letter to the Board in which it was pointed out that "nothing must be permitted to interfere with the expeditious manufacture of the experimental 5,000 amphibian ¼-ton, 4x4 trucks. . ." Figures were presented to show that no net increase in labour requirements would result from the amphibian programme, since the production schedule of Ford on the regular jeep was going to be cut 38% in accordance with a recent revision of the Army Supply Programme, resulting in the displacement of approximately 5,500 employees, or just about what would be required for the production and assembly of the amphibians. The Plant Site Board thereupon cancelled its disapproval of 20 May and cleared the contract.[38] Engineering by Ford on the hull dies was completed by the first of June and the tooling was released.[39]

The importance attached by higher authority to the problem of getting these amphibians off the assembly line without delay was again emphasised when Colonel Ingram reported to SOS Headquarters that it was anticipated by Ford that production would start 1st September and be completed by November. Even this delivery schedule could not be guaranteed, Ingram said, since "the truck has never been made before and many factors may interrupt this programme."[40] The SOS Production Branch replied that this proposed schedule made the situation "more serious" than they had thought, for even the previous understanding of SOS that 250 amphibious jeeps would be produced in August, 750 in September, 1,000 in October and 1,500 each in November and December, had been regarded as "highly unsatisfactory" by the Chief of Staff, SOS. The Quartermaster General, therefore, was directed to "take such steps as may be necessary" to the production of at least 500 amphibians in July, another 1,000 or 1,500 in August, and a similar quantity in each succeeding month until completion of the programme.[41]

General Frink immediately telegraphed Ford that every effort must be made by it to attain the result demanded by the Chief of Staff, SOS, even to the use of "overtime or such other means as are necessary to accomplish this result."[42] Ford wired back that with the use of overtime, indications were that production could begin by the end of August, and 1,000 of the amphibian jeeps probably be produced before the end of September. This information was transmitted to the SOS, 11 June, with the statement that any further information as to the bettering of this delivery schedule would be forwarded to that office.[43]

Two weeks later, Ford once more revised its production estimate as follows:

	One Shift	Two Shifts
September	Few, if any	Not practicable
October	500-1,000	Not practicable
November	1,500	3,000
December	1,500	3,000

The reason ascribed for this latest production delay was the bottleneck in some 600 dies necessary for the fabrication of the hull, none of which was common to the standard jeep. The manufacture of these dies had not started until 5 June because of the load on Ford tool production facilities occasioned by the tooling of the Ford Willow Run bomber plant and the tank production plant. However, as soon as production did get under way, the entire lot of 5,000 amphibian jeeps was expected to be produced within sixty days.[44]

A slight improvement in the estimated schedule of deliveries on the amphibian jeep was registered early in August when Ford indicated that it expected to turn out 200 in September, 1,000 in October, 2,000 in

November, and the remaining 1,800 in December.[45] But this, obviously, was still "too little and too late" to enable the amphibian jeep to contribute its share to the landing of the American Expeditionary Force on North Africa, 8 November, 1942, if that had been the purpose for which it was intended.

NOTES to CHAPTER III

1   The four-wheel steer idea was not new, having been used in the old "quad" trucks of World War I vintage. Considerable dexterity and skill on the part of the driver was required to operate these heavy quads since they frequently "responded too quickly and too much to the slightest touch on the wheel". *Army Motors*, v. 2, No. 8, 15 November 1941.

2   "Minutes of the QMC Technical Committee," 10 March 1941. The principal production difficulty, of course, was the axle bottleneck, since the four-wheel jeep required four of the constant velocity joints as against the two used in vehicles having front-wheel steering only.

3   "Minutes of the QMC Technical Committee", 10 March 1941.

4   *Ibid.*

5   *Army Motors*, v. 2, No. 8, 15 November 1941.

6   QM 095 G-C (American Bantam Motor Company), QMG to Senators Tom Stewart, Kenneth McKellar, and Representative John Jennings, Jr, 8 April 1941.

7   "Minutes of the QMC Technical Committee", 11 April 1941.

8   QM 451 (M-P) (American Bantam Co.), Brig. Gen. J.E. Barzynski to Holabird, 6 June 1941.

9   Memorandum from the QMG to the Motor Transport Division, 30 June 1941.

10   QM 451 M-P, Motor Transport to Procurement Control Branch, P&C Division, "Approval of Negotiated Contract", 30 June 1941.

11   QM 400.112 M-ES (Truck, ¼-ton, 4x4, 4-Wh. Steer), Motor Transport Subcommittee to QM Technical Committee, "Adoption of Truck, ¼-ton, 4x4, 4-wheel Steer," 4 February 1942.

12   *Ibid*, 3 February 1942.

13   "Minutes of the QMC Technical Committee", 14 March 1942.

14   Senator Robert E. Reynolds to Douglas MacKeachie, WPB, "Re: Four Wheel Steer Jeep", 9 March 1942.

15   The later conferences held with General Frink by both Fenn and Ransom have already been noted. See *supra* Chapter II.

16   QM 451 M-E (Truck, ¼-ton, 4x4, 4-Wh. Steer), General Frink to Commanding General, SOS, 17 March 1942.

17   *Ibid*, General Frink to Douglas C. MacKeachie, 17 March 1942.

18   QM 451.2 (Trucks, ¼-ton, 4x4), War Department Hdqtrs, SOS, to QMG, 1st endorsement, 24 March 1942.

19   "Minutes of the QMC Technical Committee", 10 March 1941.

20   SPQME 400.112 (¼-ton Amphibian), Motor Transport Engineering Division Report to Chief, Motor Transport Service, 11 May 1942.

21   *Ibid.*

22   "Minutes of the QMC Technical Committee", 27 June 1941; Motor Transport press release, 29 July 1941; QM 400.1141 M-ES (Truck, Amphibian, ½-ton, 4x4, Machine Gun Mounts), 7 October 1941; QMC report on Ft. Belvoir Test, 2 March 1942; "The Jeep in the Bathtub", undated draft on file in OQMG Historical Section.

23   SPQME 400.112 (Amphibian, 2½-Ton), Motor Transport Engineering Division Report to Chief, Motor Transport Service, 8 May 1942.

24   *Ibid*, Engineering Division Report to Director, Motor Transport Service, 16 June 1942; *Quartermaster Review*, "The Army's New Amphibian Truck", July-August 1943.

25   SPRMD 451.2, Hdqtrs. SOS, to QMG, "Procurement of Amphibious Trucks", 2 July 1942.

26   SPQME 400.112 (1/4-Ton, Amphibian), Motor Transport Engineering Division Report to Chief, Motor Transport Service, 11 May 1942.

27   QMC Motor Transport Progress Report, 2 July 1942.

28   SPQME 400.112 (1/4-ton Amphibian), MT Engineering Division to Chief, MT Service, 11 May 1942.

29   *Ibid.*

30   *Ibid.*

31   Chief, Motor Transport, to MT Planning Branch, 10 April 1942; QMC Motor Transport Progress Report, 2 July 1942.

32   QMM-PIR, 1/4-Ton Amphibians, MT Planning Branch to Chief, MT Service, 12 April 1942.

33   QMC Motor Transport Progress Report, 2 July 1942; Memorandum from Chief, Motor Transport, to MT Planning Branch, 10 April 1942. The later formal contract was put on a cost-plus-a-fixed-fee basis at the request of the Ford Company. QM 451 (Neg. Ford Motor Co.), W-398-qm-12937, Telegram Ford Motor Co. to Major Ralph G. Boyd, 1 May 1942; *ibid*, Major Boyd to Ford Motor Company, 19 May 1942.

34   QM 400.112, QMC Motor Transport Subcommittee to QMC Technical Committee, "Standardisation of Truck, 1/4-ton, 4x4, amphibian," 17 April 1942. The recommendation was forwarded to SOS Hdqtrs. for approval 27 May and was cleared for procurement on the first of June. On 12 June, the amphibian jeep was standardised and the QMC made responsible for its storage and issue. Monthly maintenance percentages approved were 2.1% for the Zone of the Interior and 4.2% for the Theater of Operations. The basis of issue was to be submitted separately and was to show a deletion of one standard jeep for each amphibian added to the tables. OQMG to Commanding General, SOS, "Standardisation of Truck, 1/4-ton Amphibian", 27 May 1942; 1st and 2nd Endorsements, 1 and 12 June 1942. The model standardised was the Ford Amphibian No. 3 *OQMG Daily Activity Report*, v. 10, No. 16, 17 April 1942.

35   The Motor Transport Policy Committee was established by General Frink on 21 March 1942, to consider all important motor decisions. Originally consisting of General Frink, his three Deputy Chiefs, and the Director of Planning, and meeting daily, the membership was increased in April to include the Directors of Administration, Engineering, Procurement, Storage and Issue, and Operations and Maintenance, with meetings held three times a week. Motor Transport Administrative Order No. 21, 21 March 1942; *ibid*, No. 30, 19 April 1942.

36   "Motor Transport Policy Committee Minutes", 8 May 1942.

37   SPQMP 451 (Ford Motor Company), Colonel J. Van Ness Ingram to Ford Motor Company (Attention: Mr. Roberge), 9 May 1942.

38   QM 451 (Neg. Ford Motor Co.), Brig. General J.L. Frink to WPB Plant Site Board, 22 May 1942; *ibid*, Houlder Hudgins, Chairman, Plant Site Board, to General Frink, 23 May 1942.

39   "Motor Transport Progress Report", 2 July 1942.

40   QM 451 (Neg. Ford Motor Co.), Tools for Mfg. of ¼-T 4x4 Tr, Colonel Ingram to Colonel C.J. Norman, QM Section, Production Branch, SOS, 31 May 1942.

41   *Ibid*, Lt. Col. Charles J. Norman, SOS, to QMG, 4 June 1942.

42   *Ibid*, Telegram, General Frink to Ford Motor Company, 6 June 1942.

43   *Ibid*, General Frink to SOS, 1st Endorsement, 11 June 1942.

44   "Motor Transport Progress Report", 2 July 1942.

45   QM 161 (Ford Motor Co.), Colonel Ingram to Commanding General, SOS, 4 August 1942.

CHAPTER IV

The Jeep in the Postwar World

Possible Civilian Uses: Procuring Jeeps Commercially

Ever since the initial success of the jeep, it had been recognized that a number of possible commercial adaptations of the present military type might have valuable possibilities for the recovery period after the war. The farmer, industrialist, businessman, sportsman and private citizen are all seen as likely to benefit from commercial versions of the jeep. That the public in general is aware of the jeep's post-war potentialities is evidenced by the universal interest taken in the stories of its varied feats and stunts all over the world—an interest that seems to be something more than just patriotic enthusiasm over a crack piece of American military equipment. There seems to be a personal element in this public awareness of the jeep and its performance that is quite different from the interest displayed in airplanes and tanks, for instance. Apparently, everyone would like to own a jeep after the war is over, to be used for work, sport or just fun. From different parts of the country all sorts of letters have come to the War Department and the Quartermaster Corps enquiring when and how jeeps might be acquired later from the Government or directly from the manufacturers.[1]

Nor have the manufacturers themselves been unaware of the significance of this popular interest in the jeep. The procurement struggle that took place between Bantam, Willys and Ford over the jeep contracts apparently was waged not only over the immediate orders but also over the advantageous position that would accrue to the successful bidder in any post-war competition over the manufacture of commercial variations of the jeep.[2] Ever since the lingering demise of the famed "Model T" the automobile industry has known of the need for a truly cheap and dependable "people's car" to replace it. The present so-called low-priced cars, most of them in the thousand dollar class, are really luxury models suitable for little more than pleasure driving or passenger carrying. A commercial modification of the jeep, embodying its general utility characteristics, would be useful for many purposes now requiring two or more separate vehicles. For example, it could "double in brass" for the farmer as a light tractor, a light truck, and as a car to take the family into town for shopping or to see a motion picture. Industry might take a leaf from the multiple uses to which the armed forces have put the jeep aside from strictly combat purposes,[3] and find its ruggedness and power sufficient to perform many tasks now wastefully delegated to larger and more expensive vehicles. The sportsman would find such a vehicle just the thing to reach out-of-the-way hunting and fishing spots over terrain that his present-day passenger car could not possibly negotiate. In this connection a commercial amphibian jeep might have a special appeal for him.

While any plans that Ford, Willys or Bantam might have to produce all-purpose commercial adaptions of the jeep after the war are not publicly known at this time, it is altogether likely that they will make some attempts in this direction. Recent advertisements of Willys already have attempted to capitalize on the fact that the Willys jeep is now the standard model for the armed forces, by trying to connect it with their peacetime commercial Americar. Terming the Willys Americar the "Jeep in Civies," these advertisements have proclaimed to the public that the Americar is "designed by the same engineers, built by the same trained hands, powered by the same fuel-saving Go-Devil engine as the rugged 'jeeps'. . ."[4] J.W. Frazier, president of Willys, was quoted in an April 1943 news story as foreseeing a tremendous post-war market for the jeep and predicting that it would prove "the most useful farm implement ever built." While Frazier pointed out that some changes (such as the probable elimination of the four-wheel drive) might be necessary before the vehicle could be sold commercially he also noted that "there'll be a good demand for a great many jeeps just as they are ." In all, 36 possible civilian uses for the jeep in the post-war period were envisaged by the Willys concern.

Besides being able to buy modified or unmodified jeeps after the war from the automotive industry, the public also might be allowed to purchase large numbers of the regulation military models straight from the Government. While no definite policy on the disposition of military vehicles to the public at the conclusion of the war has been determined as yet, it is quite probable that large quantities of jeeps will be available at that time for sale as surplus property. Judging from the number of jeeps already produced and being procured, as well as from the overall war requirements apt to be filled before the present conflict is over, the quantities on hand after the war are almost certain to be far in excess of peacetime military needs, even assuming a large postwar standing army with "policing" and other commitments all over the world. As of May 1942, the total jeep requirements projected through 1943 and the first six months of 1944 totalled more than 500,000.[6] Figures for July 1942 showed more than 200,000 of these procured with over 100,000 delivered.[7] Of course, many thousands of jeeps have been earmarked for lend-lease purposes,[8] and many more will have to be written-off as casualties of war, but even deducting for these, a considerable surplus should exist when the time comes to start beating swords into ploughshares.

The Jeep on the Farm

Of all the possible peacetime uses to which the jeep type of vehicle might be put after the war, probably the most important commercial application will be in the field of agriculture. The capabilities of the jeep as an all-purpose farm power unit have already been established by a series of tests conducted by the United States Department of Agriculture, 13-15 April 1942, at its Farm Tillage Machinery Laboratory located at Auburn, Alabama. In these tests the jeep proved that it could successfully substitute for a small tractor in many light ploughing and harrowing operations and otherwise demonstrated its ability to perform different types of field work. It also acquitted itself well when used as a general utility, farm transportation vehicle. R.M. Merrill, head of the laboratory, directed the experiments, and I.T. Reed and E.D. Gordon, engineers connected with the laboratory, aided in the trials. Interested Department of Agriculture observers of the tests were R.B. Gray, Chief of the Farm Machinery Division, and F.L. Teuton, Chief of the Information Division, both of the Bureau of Agricultural Chemistry and Engineering, Washington, D.C.[9]

Two regulation Army jeeps with standard four-wheel drive and using 600x16 mud and snow tread tyres were employed in the experiments. One was a Willys supplied by that company, the other being a Ford furnished by the Fourth Corps Area Quartermaster. The field tests in which they were tried included pulling practically every implement used in operations necessary to the raising of a crop. Without faltering, the jeeps ploughed the field, prepared the seed bed with double disk and tooth harrows, seeded with a grain drill and two row cotton or corn planter, and harvested a crop of rye with a mowing machine.[10]

The first operation consisted of pulling a turning plough cutting a sixteen-inch furrow, through a semi-sandy loam with the implement set to plough about seven or eight inches deep. The jeep accomplished this task without any difficulty, ploughing a strip of land about fifty feet wide and a quarter of a mile long, at a speed of from three and one half to four miles per hour. According to observers, the power exhibited by the jeep in this operation was equivalent to that of a three to four horse team, while the rate at which it pulled the plough was twice as fast as that of the team.[11]

After the field had been ploughed, it was gone over with a double disk harrow pulled by the jeep, an operation that was said to require even more power since this time the jeep was working in soft ploughed ground. With the ploughed land now thoroughly disked, a tooth harrow of two sections was employed until the soil was completely pulverized. A grain drill was then hooked to the jeep and a simulated seeding operation was gone through, following which another type of seeding machine, the two row cotton or corn planter, was operated.

Next came the most difficult test of all—pulling a double turning or gang plough, an implement carrying two ploughs each cutting a fourteen-inch furrow. With the ploughs set at approximately the same eight-inch depth, the jeep went down the field, apparently at the same rate of speed as previously, simultaneously cutting two fourteen inch furrows totalling twenty-eight inches of turned soil.

The above tests were made in a field about two miles east of Tuskegee, Alabama. When removed to rolling fields near the dairy barns of the Alabama Polytechnic Institute at Auburn, the jeep continued its demonstration as a farm power plant by pulling a lime spreader and manure spreader over and around terrace contours. The three-day experiment in farming operations then was concluded by the jeep pulling a mower to harvest a field of rye. To further demonstrate the versatility of the jeep as a handy, all-purpose farm vehicle, sacks of feed and milk cans were loaded on it to show how the farmer might use the jeep to haul his milk and other produce to the market.[12]

The official press release on the results of these tests, issued by the Department of Agriculture, disclosed that while the jeep could be considered "highly useful" as supplemental power for such farm operations, it was not suitable for the cultivation of row crops. In the opinion of R.B. Gray, one of the Department's experts who witnessed the jeep try-outs, the vehicle was both too low and too narrow for the usual row-crop cultivation jobs. It was also thought that better performance at farm work could be had from the jeep if it were furnished with a slightly lower low-gear ratio and a lower hitch for ploughing.[13]

In comparison with the usual one or two-plough small farm tractors, the jeep showed a little faster ploughing speed, but its drawbar horsepower proved to be from one to three less, its pull was about two-thirds, and its horsepower hours per gallon about a third less. When tested on the dynamometer at the Tillage Laboratory the jeep pulled 1,300 pounds with almost no wheel slippage. Additional engineering data compiled by Department of Agriculture engineers, revealed that the jeep made the following record when pulling one sixteen-inch plough cutting seven inches deep in bottom cotton land:

Drawbar horsepower	8.51
Drawbar pull	862 lbs
Speed	3.7 mph
Fuel (petrol) per hour	1.35 gal
Drawbar horsepower hours per gal	6.31
Hours per acre	1.72
Petrol per acre	2.32[14]

NOTES to CHAPTER IV

1 SPQMA 095, Sample letters on file in OQMG Historical Section. Inquirers were invariably advised "that a policy has not at this time been determined about the disposal or sale of military motor vehicles at the conclusion of the war, but you can be assured that the procedure is to give ample public notice before any such material is disposed of."

2 See *supra*, Chapters I and II.

3 For examples of these uses, many of which should be adaptable to private industry, see *supra*, Chapter I.

4 *US Federal Trade Commission Docket No. 4959* 6 May 1943.

5 *The Washington Daily News*, 13 April 1943; *The New York Times*, 10 December 1943.

6 See *supra*, Chapter II.

7 QMC Motor Transport Operations Division Compilation, 23 July 1942.

8 By March 1942, only 3,462 jeeps amounting to $3,264,781, had been actually delivered to foreign governments, Russia, China and Great Britain accounting for practically all of them. Russia received 2,185 ($2,033,864), China 920 ($879,520) and Great Britain 277 ($274,917). Three months later these figures increased noticeably, a total of 14,234 jeeps having been "floated" for lend-lease purposes by 30 June, with 11,693 more waiting in storage. (In March 1942, the SOS had informed Motor Transport that unless shipping facilities became vastly improved, it would take one and one-half years to ship abroad all of the lend-lease orders for motor trucks then on hand.) By the end of 1942, the United States had shipped to Russia alone, 81,000 military motor vehicles, a large percentage of which were jeeps. Less than one year later, in September 1943, this total had been jumped to 145,000 trucks and 25,000 jeeps. Not all of these, of course, reached their destination. Nevertheless, the thousands of jeeps and other American trucks, notably the 2½-ton, that did arrive in the Soviet Union proved enormously popular with the Russians and undoubtedly contributed materially to the solution of the vital supply problems in the Russian offensives of 1942-1943 agains the Nazis. Returning home in November 1943 from his trip to Russia, Donald M. Nelson said: "There were three American items which I found mentioned all over Russia—the Airacobra (P-39 fighter), because it kills a lot of Germans; the jeep, which they are crazy about, and the 2½-ton truck." **Status of Procurement, Defense Aid** (OQMG Statistics Branch, P&C Division), v. 16, 15 March 1942; QM 451.2 DA, Director of Operations, SOS, to Brig. General J.L. Frink, QMC, "SR 2017A", 28 March 1942; "War Aid-Reports of Vehicles Floated and in Storage", OQMG Motor Transport Depot Operations Branch, 6 July 1942; Lend-lease report to Congress by Administrator Edward R. Stettinius, Jr, for period 11 March 1941 to 31 December 1942, as carried in AP dispatch, 25 January 1943; *The Washington Post*, "Future for Russia Bright, Nelson Says", 11 November 1943; Statement of Foreign Economic Administrator Leo T. Crowley in *The Evening Star* (Washington), 16 November 1943.

9 L.P. Patterson, QMC 4th Corps Area Public Relations Branch to OQMG Motor Transport Division, 18 April 1942, on file in OQMG Historical Section.

10 *Ibid.*

11 *Ibid.*

12 *Ibid.* See *Frontispiece.*

13 US Dept. of Agriculture press release, "First of Post-War Salvage Tests Shows Jeep Could be Used on Farm", 27 May 1942.

14 *Ibid.*

War Department, Aberdeen Proving Ground, Maryland

23 June 1943

SUBJECT: Certificate re history of development of ¼-ton truck

TO: The Adjutant General, Washington DC

1. In view of articles appearing in the press, disagreements between manufacturers (Docket No. 4959, Federal Trades Commission) which have been brought to my attention, and upon the advice of senior general officers acquainted with pertinent facts, I desire to submit the attached statement, in the form of a certificate, outlining in detail the activities of the undersigned in the development of the ¼-ton truck.

2. I desire to especially emphasise the fact that the submission of this statement does not constitute an effort on my part to obtain publicity, preferential treatment or personal gain, beyond the knowledge that the record dealing with the part played by me before and during the development is complete and accurate. My part in the development covers a period of years and expenditure of personal funds and was motivated only by a desire to make a contribution to the service.

3. The body of the statement contains references to documents which are at present in storage in Louisville, Kentucky, but which can be obtained for presentation should they be required.

4. It is requested that this statement be included in the files of the War Department in the official record and the official history of this development, and also for such other purposes as the War Department may desire.

R.G. HOWIE
Col., Inf., AF
Armored Force Liaison Officer

Incl: Statement

Statement by Colonel R.G. Howie, Infantry, Armored Force,
as to the development of a small, low silhouette vehicle for military purposes

1. Recent statements in semi-official and press reports in some cases are incomplete or inaccurate. A statement by the undersigned about the background leading up to the development of the low silhouette vehicle for reconnaissance and other military purposes, known as the ¼-ton truck, appears to be needed. The following record of events, listed chronologically, for purposes of official record, has been prepared. In the event it should be advisable or necessary, the statements contained herein will be made under oath. Names of witnesses who can testify are listed.

Phase Prior to 1934

2. *a.* Having served as an infantryman before, during, and after World War I, and having been associated with automotive activities in civil life and the army, I have a personal appreciation of a difficulty which all infantrymen know: the breaking down of automatic weapons into "man loads" light enough to maintain the rate of advance of the riflemen or tank during an attack. Once an objective is gained, either by tanks or riflemen, the immediate forward displacement of automatic weapons to consolidate the position is imperative for success. There was a dire need for a low silhouette vehicle which would carry the weapon, ammunition, and at least two men to man it.

b. During the period 1931-1934, I commanded the 7th Tank Company at Fort Snelling, Minnesota. On or about 1 March 1932, I acquired an old Dodge touring car, which I used for experimental purposes to investigate the possibilities of lowering the silhouette and otherwise adapting a commercial car to the purpose desired. Considerable remodelling was done on this car, but lack of time, funds, and facilities limited the project.

Period 1934-1936

3. In the summer of 1934 I was transferred to the Infantry School, Fort Benning, Georgia, for duty as instructor in the Tank Section. During the summers of 1935 and 1936 I took leave and visited Chicago, Detroit and other places (at my own expense), investigating the field of midget racing cars and other small vehicles, including small agricultural machines, with a view to finding small power plants, power trains, axles, wheels, etc., that were commercially or otherwise available. In 1936 I discussed with Mr. John Albrecht, Field Engineer, Timken-Detroit Axle Company, the feasibility of a 4-wheel drive vehicle of the size contemplated. Mr. Albrecht furnished some detail information of dual driving axles. He also checked some of my drawing and details. During this period Col. Chas. W. Weeks, Infantry, now retired (RFD No. 1, Box 95, Dade City, Florida) encouraged me in the development of what we then termed "a snake in the grass". Colonel Weeks was relieved in 1936 by General (then Colonel) Walter C. Short (now retired). I discussed the requirement with him. He was interested and made $500.00 available to me from Book Shop funds for the experiment. Gen. Short's idea was a vehicle which could be loaded on a 1½-ton truck and visualized one with limited tactical but no strategic mobility. In this I did not concur and designed a vehicle which could operate at convoy speeds under its own power at all times. The fact that the carrier when complete was capable of being loaded on a 1½-ton truck was incidental.

Period 1937

4.   On or about 1 January, 1937, I had completed necessary drawings and details and ordered such parts as were commercially available. Due to the Ohio River floods of January-February 1937, much purchased material was delayed in shipment from Detroit and vicinity. I enlisted the services of Master Sergeant M.J. Wiley (now retired), an assistant instructor in my section of the School, to machine parts, make brackets, weld and assemble the job. By working during off hours, including Sundays, the job of assembly, started the last part of February 1937, was completed and operated for the first time in April 1937. The entire expense of the job was borne exclusively by the Book Shop and my personal funds. On 1 February 1937, General Short left Ft. Benning and therefore was not present during the construction. The Infantry Board tested the vehicle in conjunction with a series of other types with very favorable comments and a recommendation for further development. In the summer of 1937 I was ordered to the Command and General Staff School at Fort Leavenworth, Kansas. In the fall of that year the vehicle was sent to Fort Sam Houston, Texas, for a test by the Second Division, commanded by Lt. General (then Major General) Walter Krueger. General Krueger's report stated that there was a need for such a vehicle and that this one filled that need. In the fall of 1937 the Associated press and other news agencies carried photographs and a story about the vehicle. Universal News made a short of the carrier in action and used it during a weekly news reel. The undersigned has a copy of this reel and other films taken during its operation. This film includes a shot of the vehicle jumping. The following is a list of witnesses, who, among others, can testify to all or part of the above:

Lt. General Courtney H. Hodges, San Antonio, Texas
Brig. General Eugene W. Fales, Camp Roberts, California
Captain James B. Cooney, Fort Benning, Georgia
Major General Eugene M. Landrum, Alaska
Major General A.C. Gillem, Fort Knox, Kentucky
Major General Oscar W. Griswold
Major General Alexander M. Patch
Major General L. McD. Silvester, 7th Armored Division
Colonel Leo A. Bessette
Captain E. O'Hara, Fort Benning, Georgia

In December 1937, while at Fort Leavenworth, Kansas, I received a letter from General Short asking me to send him the drawings of the vehicle. This I complied with even though I was there as a student and had to devote my spare time to making a copy of the drawings which I mailed to General Short.

Period 1938–1940

5.   In June of 1938, upon graduation from the Command and General Staff School, I was ordered to return to Fort Benning, Georgia, for duty. On my way I visited Washington, DC. While there, I was informed that General Short had applied for a patent on this vehicle. Upon arrival at Fort Benning, I was informed by Lt. General (then Colonel) Hodges and Major General (then Lt. Col.) Landrum that a request by General Short for a patent had been referred to the Infantry School through the Chief of Ordnance, and that it had been returned with the information to the effect that the design of this vehicle was mine and should be so recorded. Later that year a patent was issued for this vehicle in the names of General Short, the undersigned, and, in view of circumstances, I included the name of Sergeant Wiley. During 1938 and 1939 the vehicle was demonstrated by the undersigned to many people, military and civilian, including Mr. Bernard Baruch, but no concrete plans were made by the War Department or others for the production of vehicles in volume.

6. It was used by the 29th Infantry for several months in tests, maneuvers and demonstrations, and by 1940 had been operated over 4,000 miles, most of it cross country, and its practical usefulness had been demonstrated.

7. In March 1940, Mr. Jos. W. Frazer, President, Willys-Overland Motors, and Mr. Delmar C. Roos, Vice-President and Chief Engineer, Willys-Overland Motors, visited Fort Benning and witnessed a demonstration. General Short asked me to turn over drawings to Mr. Roos as he, General Short, advanced the idea of having the Willys-Overland Motors build a production model commercially for the British, inasmuch as the American Army did not appear to be doing much with it. These drawings were given to Mr. Roos at that time.

8. In June 1940, while I was on maneuvers with the Provisional Tank Brigade in Louisiana, I received a radiogram from the Chief of Infantry directing me to proceed to Butler, Pennsylvania, to the Bantam Motor Car Company and to bring with me the drawings of the "Howie Carrier". Upon arrival at Butler, I met an Infantry, Ordnance and Quartermaster Committee, who informed me that 70 vehicles were to be contracted for and that I was to turn over my drawings and remain with the Bantam Company to formulate plans and specifications for the new vehicle. This vehicle was to be based on the characteristics and engineering data of the "Howie Carrier", incorporating 4-wheel drive, with a capacity of 3 passengers. The Board also asked me to form an opinion as to whether or not the Bantam Company was capable of building the vehicle if awarded a contract. At that time the plant was not operating. The Board remained at Butler one

day. During the day the plant was inspected and conferences held with Mr. Fenn, President, Mr. Payne, who was interested in negotiating the contract with the War Department, and Mr. Probst, the Chief Engineer. Before leaving Butler that night the Board directed me to remain at the Bantam Plant as long as necessary to complete plans and specifications so that the Bantam Company could proceed if and when directed. Mr. Robert F. Brown, civilian engineer, Holabird Quartermaster Depot, a member of the Board (now with Development Branch TAC) remained with me for approximately two days, during which time we discussed engineering features of the vehicle. I remained at the plant for approximately 7 additional days, during which time I turned over drawings, phots and other data of the Howie Carrier to the Bantam Company, wrote and submitted specifications for the new vehicle. During this period it was the desire of the Bantam Company to use many of their standard production parts and unit assemblies, without change. It was not without some discussion that I was able to convince them that the vehicle must be engineered completely as a new vehicle, and that the success of the job depended upon the inclusion of those characteristics, such as floatation, power to weight ratio, angles of approach and departure, size of axles, wheels, tyres, frame, wheelbase, tread, and power transmission, all in proper relation to each other, as were proven in the Howie carrier and which gave it cross country agility and stamina. These characteristics were incorporated into the specifications. During this period an engineer of the Spicer Corp. was called in, and a drawing of a front wheel drive, prepared by me with the aid of Mr. Albrecht (see par. 3), was given him.

9. In July 1940, I was transferred to Fort Knox, Kentucky, as executive officer, Armored Force School, which detail precluded further participation in the production.

10. I desire to emphasize the fact that my part in the development covering a period of years, most of it at my own expense, was given merely as a desire on my part to make a worthwhile contribution to the service. There never was at any time any idea or desire on my part for publicity, financial gain, or preferential treatment. Since the development has resulted successfully and since public statements have been made which are slightly at variance with the above, or incomplete, the above statement is made with a view to clarification and recognition of the facts as stated.

11. I certify that the above statements are true and accurate to the best of my knowledge and belief.

R.H. HOWIE
Col., Inf., AF
Armored Force Liaison Officer
Aberdeen Proving Ground, Maryland

COMMENTS AND CORRECTIONS

The following comments and corrections were made by Col. E.S. Van Deusen on 22 May 1946 after a careful perusal of this study.

Colonel Van Deusen, a graduate in engineering of the University of Michigan, resigned his position with one of the large automobile manufacturers to become a lieutenant in World War I. He remained in the Army and, shortly after the Motor Transport Corps was abolished and the function vested in the Quartermaster Corps, he was assigned to the Motor Transport Branch of the Transportation Division. There he remained until the middle of 1942, when he was transferred, with Motor Transport, to the Ordnance Department and became a member of the staff of the Office of the Chief of Ordnance, Detroit. During the period of the emergency and until his transfer to the Ordnance Department he was responsible for both engineering and procurement; during the war years with Ordnance he was the principal adviser on transport vehicles to the Chief of Ordnance, Detroit. There is no one, therefore, better qualified by training and experience to criticise this study.

General Comment

"In general, a very good presentation, except as noted . . . [below]."

Specific Comments

Page

11   This picture is *not* one of the first 70 units built by Bantam, but looks like one of the 1,500 built subsequently.

15   The engine used by Bantam in the first 70 vehicles, also used in Bantam's subsequent production *was not* development by Continental Motors as a result of this project. The engine was selected from Continental Motors Corporation's line of standard production, a 112 cu. in. engine which had previously been quite widely used for small power plant use in generator units, pump units and air compressor applicators, with a very few minor modifications to adapt it to the automotive use.

22   This is not completely true. The record will show that, despite the provisions of the Act of 2 July 1940, and the efforts of QMC to secure vehicle standardisation under its provisions, competitive bidding, although of the informal type, was continued as a requirement for award under rulings of the OASW for a long time thereafter. The fact that some modicum of standardisation was secured through continuation of awards to certain makers for a certain type of vehicle was not due per se to any action by the War Department as much as it was a result of favourable price quotations by the makers of the particular vehicles which became the accepted "standard" and which later were procured by negotiation.

40   There is a point which is not understood by many people not cognisant of the organisation and methods of operation in the motor industry. Bantam had only *one plant*. Ford and General Motors (both Chevrolet and Y T & C Mfg. Co.) had several plants. Thus work assigned to Chev. (as example) was not putting all the eggs in one basket as it would be in case of either Bantam or Willys. Although not included in the written record which covers QMC efforts to have the order for 16,000 units late in 1941 made to Ford, the fact that Willys had but one plant, as opposed to several widely dispersed Ford plants *was* a factor considered in making the QMG's recommendation for award of this first big order to Ford.

The Alexandria, Va. Branch office of Ford Motor Co. was *the* office through which *all* US Army and Ford Motor contract matters were handled at this time. The Alexandria office was acting as agent for the Ford main office at Dearborn, Mich., in dealing with the Army. Other Branch offices were not involved.

Timing and dates are wrong here. The Hofheins proposal was made early in 1940, and he demonstrated in 1941, shortly after initiation of the NDRC project for the ¼-ton amphibian. The 2½-ton amphibian (DUKW) project was initiated in April of 1942, *after* acceptance of the ¼-ton NDRC amphibian as being satisfactory for use.